THE MASTERPIECE
OF THE WILDERNESS
Journeys of a Warrior Poet

D1531373

DEANNA DEERING

voice ministries

Voice Ministries, Inc.
58300 Ash Road Osceola, Indiana 46561
www.voiceministries.com

Copyright ©2003, 2005 Voice Ministries, Inc.

First Printing: May 2003

Second Printing: October 2005

Printed in the United States of America.

Photography by Joshua Petrillo. Author photo by Shirley Ballard.

This book is printed on acid free paper.

ISBN: 0-9773964-0-1

THANK YOU

My thanks and gratitude to all the following:

My father and mother, Richard and Sylvia Komyatte, who taught me to seek the Lord at a young age and revealed His love through lives of selflessness and sacrificial giving. You always had a home open for me to return to — no matter what I was going through — you were there for me with unconditional love.

My brother and sister, Paul and Kristin, who have loved me through many life-transitions — never to turn away.

My sister-in-law, Linda Deering, who served me by watching my two sons so that I could seek the Lord in a deeper way. This could never be repaid. Thank you for your sacrifice.

My friend and brother, Denny Rogers, who sacrificially interceded during my hardest times. Your love and genuine concern carried me through some darks days of the soul.

My friend and brother, Corey Stark — one who desires to embrace the cross fully. As you said, "When we get together, we always end up laughing, no matter how painful the circumstances may seem."

TABLE OF CONTENT

FOREWARD

It has been nearly four years now that I have been receiving prophetic impressions from the Lord. Although I always loved to write and believed it was a gifting from the Lord, I was a stranger to receiving writings from Him as if He were speaking to me. While we live in a nature that is steeped in imperfections, the voice of the Lord can break through with a truth and love so far above our ordinary level of existence. This is His gift to us — a gift given for the purpose of knowing Him more, loving Him more, and understanding His heart more.

At the prompting of others, I am sharing these writings, along with my devotional writings. While the voice of the Lord is pure and true, it comes through a vessel that is not pure and not wholly true by the Lord's standards. Therefore, I encourage you to separate the wheat from the chaff. My utmost desire is that you hear Him, not me, speak to you personally from these writings. When He does this, the purpose of the book will have been fulfilled. My desire is that you will be closer to Him because He drew you into intimacy through words that drew me into deeper love with Him. Regardless of our stage in the journey, we all hold one consistent need: to know Him more, to love Him more deeply, and to understand His heart.

As I have journeyed with the Lord throughout the course of this book, He has led me to share these thoughts. There is a sense where we receive our life from the Lord, in order for it to be given away. The journey is the path towards healing. Until we make this journey, we are fragmented, wounded individuals trying to live our lives in the best way we know how. The present world system is in the hands of the evil one, and every person born into this life will experience oppression in varying degrees. Although flesh and blood will be used as vessels of oppression and pain, our struggle is against the authorities and powers of this dark world and against spiritual forces of evil in the heavenly realms.

The awesome news is that God is in the process of redemption! He is always pouring forth His love, redeeming our inner man, releasing us to walk in faith and surrender, rather than in fear and control. For truly, fear and control are two of the greatest obstacles we encounter in our fallen nature. We will be molded by these two forces or we will take our stand against them. But in order to take our stand, the Lord must "undo" much that has been done. He will give us our new identity in Him, but we must make the journey to receive it. A new identity takes process and preparation. This is the journey.

Be willing to face the journey. Be willing to face the truth and embrace it. God wants to release His people into true inner freedom — not false freedom, which is the freedom we grow up embracing. False freedom is the end result of trying to free ourselves from the inner bondage or oppression we acquire simply by being born in a fallen world. How many of us are born into a family or a community where the inner spirit is nourished, and the inner fire is fanned, so that we run free with the spirit of the Living God in true liberty, in true conformity to the purpose for which we were born?

Never underestimate the power of God. He can do radical things in you, in your heart, and in your world. Things that would seem to take hundreds of years, He can accelerate within an amazingly short period. My prayer is that you glimpse for just a moment how much He truly loves you and how much He desires to be with you.

After He gives us our self as a gift of healing and wholeness, He invites us to lay our self down in response. We receive our life in order to give it away. To pick up our cross is to lose our life for His sake, so we can enter into the true life He came to give: a life which is not our own, but which is His life. From the cross come pain and death, but the cross is never the final word for those who are in Christ Jesus. Resurrection life is the final word, and from that life proceeds an *agape* love and an unquenchable freedom that we can know in no other way. The cross will always confound the wisdom of this world and it will also cause terror among the enemy's camps. For once we all start loving our lives not unto death, we will make an invincible army in the hands of the risen Lord.

We will never be fully free until we love the way that God Himself loves. His cross is the greatest demonstration of love that has ever existed. If we love the way that God loves, we will be embracing the cross. I pray that you would be led to embrace it. I pray that the eyes of your heart would be enlightened to understand how His cross is meant to work a definite process of transformation in your earthly life. The cross is his invitation to dwell in Him more and more deeply, to experience His love and His heart for this world which He will ultimately redeem and reclaim as His own.

The more you come to live by the cross of Jesus Christ, the more you will live by the power of His love. We are entering a time in history when we must live by the power of His love. While darkness is rapidly increasing, He is calling out for His people to radically live by the power of His love. We must know His cross in the very depths of our being. This will be the light that we carry forward as we enter the battle that lies ahead. Isaiah 60:1-3 says, "Arise, shine, for your light has come, and the glory of the Lord rises upon you. See, darkness covers the earth and thick darkness is over the peoples, but the Lord rises upon you and His glory appears over you. Nations will come to your light, and kings to the brightness of your dawn." There is no limit to His love and His life that is available for us who believe! Let us together advance His kingdom of light into the kingdom of darkness, and reveal it for what it is.

In Christ's love,

Deanna Deering

PROPHETIC
WRITINGS

MASTERPIECE OF THE WILDERNESS

Reward for the Steadfast

There is a great reward coming for those who persevere. Hold fast, My child. Be diligent in seeking My presence. The flesh always screams in pain as it is being pressed through the narrow door. But do not be dismayed.

In this world, I was the only Perfect One. Yet, I am calling you to higher levels of perfection. This is a process for all My children. The path I hold for My dear ones is a steep one and the joy that follows suffering may seem to be far away. Rejoice, however, in this: the promise is sure. As you are faithful to seek Me, and fervent in your desire for "more," I will hold out your reward.

Take heart. You will be like the prisoner who brings forth very beautiful music from within confining walls — because you are My prisoner, no one else's.

Those who are called are trained quite rigorously. Do not lament because you are there right now. Rather, rejoice! You are in the final stages of preparation. Your focus on Me must be ever so precise now. Simplify. Simplify all aspects of your life. Then you will hear Me more clearly.

All Else Follows My Heart

I am teaching you constancy, stability. Your love for Me must be so pure that it is not affected by circumstances ... good or bad. Your emotions must be submitted to your spirit in such a way that you are able to walk through ALL events with the certainty that I am Sovereign. If you weep, weep with My heart. If you rejoice, let it be rejoicing with Me. Seek My heart; all else will follow.

JOURNEYS OF A WARRIOR POET

12

Going Deep

Resist the surface. Dwell in the depths. That means you must resist busyness, resist "activity," resist focusing on needs — both your own and those of many others.

I am the Need-Meeter, and I will give to you abundantly more than you can imagine … if you will only allow Me. But first you must, at all costs, resist the surface.

I am calling you into the depths, for this is where I am waiting to give you more. This is where I empower you to go out. And once I have empowered you, I send you out to do what I came to do. Your work will not resemble busyness, nor will it be burdensome. It will carry My authority to heal and to set the captives free.

Resist the SURFACE.
Dwell in
the DEPTHS.

I empower only those who are resolute in seeking Me first. Those who forsake their self to Me, who forsake the "good" for the best, who forsake the temptations of the flesh, will find Me whom they seek.

But your seeking must not only be whole-hearted, it must have an element of forcefulness about it. I told you that, from the beginning, the Kingdom of Heaven has been forcefully advancing, and that forceful men and women lay hold of it. (Matthew 11:12). What do you think this means? Do you have any idea what resistance you will meet when you set out to go deep in Me? And do not make the mistake of thinking that "forceful" has to do with your strength or your personality. The weakest saint can lay claim to My kingdom more forcefully and effectively than some of the strongest ones out there. (Philippians 3:7-8).

"Forceful" implies a resoluteness that refuses to look aside or within, but rather, aggressively fixes its eyes upon Me in the midst of all the distractions that are thrown upon it. Self-love, the manipulations of others, and the clever schemes of the enemy (Ephesians 6:10-20) will keep you in a whirlwind if you do not take an aggressive stand with your will (Ephesians 6). I ache for you when you get caught up on the surface.

You must be like the man who found a treasure hidden in a field. In his joy he hid it again, went and sold everything he had, and bought the field. It was his joy that led him to give up everything for the sake of the hidden treasure. (Matthew 13:44).

I promise you this joy, if you will open the door on which I knock. It is deep within you, and only those with the eyes of their heart open can even hear My voice calling. I am searching to and fro across the earth for friends who will carry out My commands, but it will only be done by dwelling in the depths where I am.

I am calling you to Me. Do not forsake My voice. Do not forfeit My love.

Within

"Too many of my people are looking outward, and the answer is within. I must turn their eyes within — for healing, for crucifixion, for inner transformation. Then their eyes can truly see outward — for the gaze is pure.

The Primary Purpose of the Desert

When I allure you into the desert, I have one primary purpose at work. I desire to become your only lover. In the desert you will discover the depth and the desperation of your thirst like never before. And yet, you will come to be satisfied to the measure of all My fullness.

Though you may be lonely, though you may be in deep pain, though you may be utterly shattered in your outer nature, you will come to know Me. And to know Me is to know My love for you. One taste of My love in your deep, dry thirst will change your cold and crusty heart forever.

Little by little, My love poured out upon and within you will change you. It is My love that draws you out from the temptations of the world and draws you into the fire of the desert. A man or woman comes face to face with his or her self in the desert. And you must face yourself, if you want to truly come to know Me. Knowing Me in My thoughts, in My words, and in My deeds is one thing, but knowing Me in My heart is another!

> Love which springs from your own desires and your own convenience is a stronghold.

If this goal is accomplished in you, then you will be able to love others with the love that is in My heart. My desire is that you will see the love that is in your heart in relation to the love that is in Mine. Love which springs from your own desires and your own convenience is a stronghold you must be delivered from. This love is a poor imitation of My holy, *agape* love.

But you must also know this: I only keep you in the desert if you desire to embrace the fire that My judgments bring to all that is not holy within you. If you want out, I will let you out. But such an aborted release will not bring the fullness of celebration that it was intended to bring. My purpose is to make you ONE with Me in the desert, to bring you into a union that will consecrate yourself onto My will, and to decree certain changes that will forever be within the marrow of your soul.

Ah — then I will delight in bringing other desert-lovers to you. Desert-lovers are those who have made the core of their being and the foundation of their purpose to be ministry to Me. They will come to Me for no other reason than to lavish their love upon Me, knowing that this is why they were created. They will not come to receive anything — not even My glory or My presence. They will come to lay all that is within them at any particular moment at My feet.

Do you desire to be My desert-lover? Bring me your all, wanting nothing in return. Knowing Who I am, knowing who you are: this is the union that I desire to have with you, My beloved.

SCRIPTURE
"Therefore I am now going to allure her; I will lead her into the desert and speak tenderly to her … In that day," declared the Lord, "you will call Me 'my Husband'; you will no longer call me 'my Master.' I will remove the names of the Baals from her lips; no longer will their names be invoked … I will betroth you to Me forever; I will betroth you in righteousness and justice, in love and compassion. I will betroth you in faithfulness, and you will acknowledge the Lord." (Hosea 2:14, 16-17, 19-20, NIV)

"I will sprinkle clean water on you, and you will be clean; I will cleanse you from all your impurities and from all your idols. I will give you a new heart and put a new spirit in you; I will remove from you your heart of stone and give you a heart of flesh. And I will put My Spirit in you and move you to follow My decrees and be careful to keep My laws." (Ezekiel 36:25-27, NIV)

Striving

All manner of striving must cease, My child. Don't you see that there is no one who can teach you this? All over the world, My elect are hearing that they must learn to abide and enter My rest.

What many believers call RESTING IN THE LORD is actually a state of passivity.

But do not be fooled by the counterfeit. What many believers call "resting in the Lord" is actually a state of passivity. The rest I am calling you to is a state in which man learns to rest from his own efforts, his own strength, his own desires and ideas. In this state, he becomes much more alive to My Spirit within. My Spirit, then, will lead him to action, not activity. This position of rest produces Spirit-inspired action. It is far different than either activity or passivity. It is the rest wherewith I have called you.

Approval

There is a major difference between a life that knows it is already approved and a life that is seeking approval. The one experiences peace; the other, unrest. It takes time for Me to move you from one state to the next, much time spent in My presence, receiving My love, which is reaching out to renew your mind and heal your soul. How few of My children know they are approved by Me!

Never the Victim

Embrace all happenings with love. Resist any urge to blame people, places, or things. All events happen according to My hand. I bring all things to work for the good of My beloved children. In all events, I am teaching you many things. My true children will earnestly seek to learn all that they can from Me. They seek and trust.

You can even learn through events that are caused by the sin or disobedience of another person. You may seem to be the victim, but this is not the truth. I was the Lamb Who was slain. All thought I was done — including My primary foe. But, to the contrary, My Father's love was brought to a culmination in the cross. View your life in this manner: you are the victim only if you refuse to enter into fellowship with Me.

> You are the victim only if you refuse to enter into fellowship with Me.

Separation

There is going to be a people who have no ties to the world, who have given up everything and endured the hottest fires. They are ready to go anywhere, to say anything, to be my hands and feet. They will soar like eagles because they truly have left this world, and they will glow with my love because they have submitted to my purification and no longer is their flesh a veil over my presence within them.

My Food, Your Food

Remember, I have known you since the beginning of time. I will always know you. I created you by My very breath. I designed your frame for special purposes unique to you.

I am the Holy One, the Living Word of God, the Bread of Life come down from Heaven. As I told My disciples, "My food is to do the will of Him Who sent Me," so your food will be to do My will.

Bread from Heaven, then, becomes your nourishment in direct relation to your willingness and your obedience to walk in My will. Many of My children are malnourished because they haven't learned what is their proper food. They believe that My word alone will feed them. But remember, I said that My food is TO DO the will of Him Who sent Me.

> I designed your frame for special purposes unique to you.

SCRIPTURE
"Therefore, my beloved, as you have always obeyed, not as in my presence only, but now much more in my absence, work out you own salvation with fear and trembling." (Philippians 2:12)

"For it is God Who works in you both to will and to do for His good pleasure." (Philippians 2:13)

Pursue the Highest Call

If you must be pushed into a tight spot in order to believe, then so be it. Just believe. Whatever it takes, I will work My work within you. You have asked for nothing less. It is in those moments of union with Me that covenants are made, promises are given, visions are revealed.

You must, however, walk out these covenants in your body of flesh. This is where the testing begins: the frustrations, the impatience, the discouragement, the doubt. I, the Son of God, the Perfect One, learned obedience through suffering. How much more My children need to!

> You determine how high you will go.

And yet, as you persevere through all the discouragement of the flesh, you will climb to higher heights in the Spirit. So persevere and believe. Perseverance and faith must go hand-in-hand. These two commands I give to you in order that you may stand firm until the end.

It is not the initial treasures that require strength and determination. My beloved ones are being fought right now to give up pursuit of their HIGHEST callings. Many will not be guilty of turning their backs on Me; they will be guilty of giving up the pursuit of My highest call. My highest call will require your ALL. It will require single-minded focus, strength to press in at all costs, and denial of the flesh to a great degree.

The promise is there. I am never lacking in My Word. But in order to accept My offer, you must grasp hold of it. Do you understand? My highest call must be won by you just as intensely as the

Olympian pursues the gold with rock-solid commitment and unshakable determination.

Those who run to enjoy the race will not win. Those who run to be part of the race will not win. Only the one with single-eyed focus and rigorous, relentless determination will win. Never mistake the race as being against one another. The race is against the possibilities I lay before you. You determine how high you will go.

SCRIPTURE
"I press on toward the goal to win the prize for which God has called me heavenward in Christ Jesus." (Philippians 3:14, NIV)

"Do you know that in a race all the runners run, but only one gets the prize? Run in such a way as to get the prize. Everyone who competes in the games goes into strict training. They do it to get a crown that will not last; but we do it to get a crown that will last forever. Therefore, I do not run like a man running aimlessly; I do not fight like a man beating the air. No, I beat my body and make it my slave so that after I have preached to others, I myself will not be disqualified for the prize." (1 Corinthians 9:24-27, NIV)

Oneness

There are certain barriers you must break through in order to come into oneness with Me. Divine union is what I seek in the lives of every single one of My children. Union of the soul with Myself, My heart, My life. This is impossible to achieve on your own. It is a divine work given by Me, but initiated by the soul's request.

Oneness. What power rests in Oneness.

Trust Me to Make You Mature

Come to Me because you trust Me, and because you now know that only I can give you life. I have been working in you. You have to trust Me to make you mature and complete, lacking nothing (James 1:4). What an incredible word, that you shall not lack anything! That means you will be able to walk through, enter, and come up against everything that lies ahead. And there is a lot that lies ahead.

You desire to be used by Me, but you have human hands and a human heart. I've got to make you less dependent on your "good ideas" and more in tune with My thoughts, My love, My purpose.

Every child of Mine, because he or she is born into this fallen world, secretly seeks to receive recognition and affirmation from without. There should be no shame in admitting it, for it is part of your human nature. Other people help you feel good, needed, purposeful, loved.

> You have to trust Me to make you mature and complete, lacking nothing.

But dear one, you are on a training ground. I want you to desire and to seek only My affirmation, My approval. As a human, your temptation is to do what is "measurable." An obvious good work is noticeable to other people, and helps to satisfy your own inner need for identity. In that way, good works can keep you far away from Me. Every sincere believer needs to be broken of this natural inclination. (John 15:1-2). It is so easy to receive joy when you do something that brings personal contentment. But don't you see that My job is to pull you out of everything you can say you ever "did"? Your contentment must rest in knowing that nothing you could ever do can bring you contentment.

You have to trust that your peace and joy is only in My purpose and in My plan. And when you are ready to let go of the "measurable," I can open up what is "immeasurable" to you.

SCRIPTURE
"Now to Him who is able to do exceedingly abundantly above all that we ask or think, according to the power that works in us." (Ephesians 3:20)

Further References: Matthew 5:48; Mark 8:33-35; Luke 8:11-15; John 12:25, 14:27; 2 Corinthians 7:1; Colossians 4:12; Philippians 3:12-16

Entering in the Deeper Life

Why are you holding on to everything, when I have told you, "It is better to give than to receive"? And I do not mean just money, or even your time; I mean your opinions, your strong-mindedness, your desires, your personal satisfactions. Do you know how much power and strength lies dormant within you as a body? But, because you all hold on to yourselves so much, you aren't entering in.

I mean for Paul's words in Galatians 2:20 to be a reality: "I have been crucified with Christ; it is no longer I who live, but Christ lives in me; and the life which I now live in the flesh I live by faith in the Son of God, Who loved me and gave Himself for me." What would happen if just a few of My children grasped this reality, and not only for one second, or one hour, or one whole day, but for a complete inner transformation!

One of the reasons My church is so ineffective is because this concept never takes hold for very long. It may take hold for a while, but before a foundation of power and effectiveness can arise, the evil one comes in and sweeps away the little fires of revival almost as soon as they begin to burn.

I told you it would be hard. I told you that following Me means death to your self. You listen to these words and you speak them to others, but are you ready to live them? If I could get a group of believers who are living these words — and loving one another, bearing one another's burdens,

> I told you that following Me means death to yourself.

interceding for one another, and standing together in prayer and support when the enemy comes in on one of their lives — WHAT I COULD DO!

I walked the path; I spoke to you all the words you need to know. Now you must decide: on what level are you going to follow Me?

I counsel you to seek after that DEEPER life, that ULTIMATE purpose for living. You'll never be satisfied until you do!

SCRIPTURE
"Enter by the narrow gate; for wide is the gate and broad is the way that leads to destruction, and there are many who go in by it. Because narrow is the gate and difficult is the way which leads to life, and there are few who find it." (Matthew 7:13-14)

"For I have no one like-minded, who will sincerely care for your state. For all seek their own, not the things which are of Christ Jesus." (Philippians 2:20-21)

Further References: Matthew 16:24-25, 18:3-4, 19:30; Luke 14:25-33; Acts 7:51; Philippians 3:18-21

Spirit of Control

What does your life testify to? Does it reveal My strength in weakness … or your weakness trying desperately to be strong?

You may be able to fool others; you may even fool yourself. But I know what is happening. There is nothing in life you can do without Me.

Sometimes My people act as though they need to prove their strength to Me. I created you to be vessels for Me, letting My strength pour into you … and out through you.

I know the human heart. I know its ability to deceive itself. The walls of pride are thick. Control is a demon. Why do My people continually submit themselves to such a force? There is nothing so stifling to My Spirit as this insidious spirit of control.

> I know the human heart. I know its ability to deceive itself.

[January 9, 1997: I believe that when I received this writing, God impressed upon me that it was applicable to every believer in His body. Control, pride, and deceit operate in various levels within His body; ranging from obvious "mega-doses" in a person's life, to mild doses hidden to the human eye and ability to discern, except through the Spirit. Whether mild or mega, they all block the flowing of His Spirit, and prevent the freedom in communion with our brothers and sisters that is necessary if we desire to see God's kingdom advanced. Paul says that the Lord is the Spirit, and where the Spirit of the Lord is, there is freedom. (2 Corinthians 3:17). It is for freedom that Christ has set us free. (Galatians 5:1).]

No human is exempt from the spirit of control. Our human nature, from the very beginning of time, wanted control. The question is: how does it operate in your life? In one life it may be obvious and ugly, but in another it may disguise itself in the form of doing good. If we want to move God's kingdom forward in this time and in this place, then we must repent of all forms of control, receive forgiveness, and seek Jesus' absolute total control of our selves and the lives of all those He has placed around us.

Troubled Hearts

Let not your heart be troubled.
Let not your soul be dismayed.
For My plan for you is not finished.
In fact, it has only begun.
Remember that My time is not your time,
And My ways are not yours.
The world's view of progress holds no weight with Me,
For I will judge you by your heart,
And by your ability to let Me be your Lord.

Do not be fooled by the world's wooing
And try to rely on your own works,
For you will fail, unless you realize that
Your efforts apart from Me are futile,
And come back to Me in weakness,
So that I may be your strength.
And so I may flood your soul with all the Light,
The Grace, and the Love you have always sought for.
Stop your seeking.
I am here at your door.
All you need to do is open it.

Stand Firm

(2 Chronicles 20:3ff NIV): "Alarmed, Jehoshaphat resolved to inquire of the Lord, and he proclaimed a fast for all Judah ... 'We have no power to face this vast army that is attacking us. We do not know what to do, but our eyes are upon you' ... 'This is what the Lord says to you: "Do not be afraid or discouraged because of this vast army. For the battle is not yours, but God's ... You will not have to fight this battle. Take up your positions, stand firm, and see the deliverance the Lord will give you ... Have faith in the Lord your God and you will be upheld!"'"

> It seems as though Job's suffering was purposeless. But I came to confound the wise.

"Inquire of Me" — You are correct in doing so. You have no power in yourself. Do not be fooled into thinking there is something you missed or left undone. The enemy would love to have you looking within yourself and living with the feeling that you are not okay. The enemy wants you to think there must be something wrong with you, or you would not be suffering like this. The enemy would convince you that you do not have enough faith, or you have an area of disobedience in your life that must be surrendered.

Remember, Job suffered when his friends tried to reason out why he was suffering. But it was because he was found righteous that I allowed Satan to buffet him.

Many unbelievers think, "If this is your God, I don't want anything to do with Him." It seems (only to your human eye, of course) as though Job's suffering was purposeless. But I came to confound the wise. And time and time again people write books that try to put Me into a formula in which they make sense out of how I work.

The focus is not on you. The power is not in your doing. The power is in Me. Keep your eyes on Me; the battle is Mine. To you, the army is vast — you cannot see through it. But you will not have to fight this battle. Do not be discouraged. Stand firm and you will see the deliverance I will give you.

SCRIPTURE
"Because he has set his love upon Me, therefore I will deliver him; I will set him on high, because he has known My name. He shall call upon Me, and I will answer him; I will be with him in trouble; I will deliver him and honor him. With long life I will satisfy him, And show him My salvation." (Psalm 91:14-16)

Further References: Job 1:1, 8, 23:10-12; Psalm 9-11, 22, 26:16-22, 27:11-14, 28:6-9

No Reputation to Defend

There is a great trial going on across the land of My beloved. It is a trial of the heart. Remember, My love, that the final death is the death of reputation. Let people think you are weak, fragile, unable to handle life's problems. What does man's opinion matter to you? You know that no man can judge you for what you are undergoing. Yet, in their weakness, people will. It will always be easier to judge than to love. Remember this.

I give you meekness to endure the humiliation that comes from false judgment. I endured the most tarnished of reputations, yet spoke not a word of defense, for I knew My Father would glorify Me when it was His time. I am glorified in weakness. I ask you, am I glorified in strength? I know too well, dear one, that the church today sees weakness as weakness. But I see weakness as My opportunity to pour grace and glory all over your feeble frame. So you are weak. Blessings to Me! So people are judging you. Blessings to Me!

Who is willing to endure shame by My hand? I will revolutionize the very definition of strength in the western church. Those who think they are strong right now will be appalled at the unveiling of their weakness; self-righteousness is so easily obscured by strength. My people, wake up! I have called the weak. I have called the sick. I have called those who have no reputation to defend. Will you open your eyes? Will you open your ears? "He who loves his life will lose it, and he who hates his life in this world will keep it for eternal life." (John 12:25). I ask you: what do you hate? What do you love?

SCRIPTURE
Further References: Psalm 27; 2 Corinthians 12:9-10; Matthew 5:3-12

Only One Thing Matters

You must not allow yourself to be in a rush. There is no way you can be led by the Spirit when you are in a hurry. Walk, don't run, in the Spirit. You say, "There is much that needs to be done, and these are real responsibilities." But there is only one thing that matters. By doing this "one thing," you will accomplish more than you ever could have by doing the "many things" first. But not to the visible eye, of course; the results are first received in the spiritual realm, then revealed in the natural.

Without Me and My Spirit, you cannot possibly carry out My commands. I have many plans for you, but you can only walk in them through your spirit. Taking time to seek Me brings your flesh into obedience, for it inherently desires quick results. Your outer man has taken many years to be formed. When you set out to seek Me, your outer man will be pressed into submission to My Spirit. Such a process takes time, and it can be very excruciating.

This is why many will opt for busyness and allow the visible results to deceive them. My loved one, do not allow yourself to be deceived! Wide is the door through which many will travel. I'm coaxing you. I'm calling you. Allow Me to have all of you, so I can take you through the narrow door.

SCRIPTURE
"Now it happened as they went that He entered a certain village; and a certain woman named Martha welcomed Him into her house. And she had a sister called Mary, who also sat at Jesus' feet and heard His word. But Martha was distracted with much serving, and she approached Him and said, 'Lord, do You not care that my sister has left me to serve alone? Therefore tell her to help me.' And Jesus answered and said to her, 'Martha, Martha, you are worried and troubled about many things. But one thing is needed, and Mary has chosen that good part, which will not be taken away from her.'" (Luke 10:38-42)

No Such Thing as Failure

You are not a failure, My child. You have your mind focused on the highest goal, and that is why you feel you've fallen so short of what is possible.

But I do not come to bring you condemnation. I am touched by your desire to bring to Me your best. My chosen ones are called to set their minds on Me and to aspire after My very best. I only give to those who desire Me with a thirst that simply cannot be quenched by anything earthly. But rest today in this Truth: you reside in a human vessel, and until you are with Me in My heavenly home, you walk in the possibility of falling short of all I offer you to walk in. But this Truth should not cause you to shrink back or to aspire after lesser things. It should cause you to abide in Me with greater certainty of just how desperately you need Me. I treasure this attitude of heart.

> You are not a failure, My child.

Response Reveals

When you are at your very lowest and someone hurts you, through ridicule, judgment, or just plain insensitivity, and you respond in your heart with compassion toward this person, then you will know that you truly have more of My heart inside of you than your own limited human heart.

My Joy

Today I speak to you, "Joy." Joy, pure and simple. Joy, strong and sturdy. This is one of My greatest treasures, and when received, it is unspeakable and unsurpassed.

Many are the trials you have been going through, and many have been the difficult lessons. Now is the time for you to receive your reward. A mere glimpse of what awaits you is enough—enough to renew your strength, enough to fan your fire, enough to make you hunger for more. This is the intimacy I long to give, but only to those who are willing to suffer the way.

"Blessed is he who comes in the name of the Lord." Blessed are you who dwell with Me, persistently pursuing Me, despite all obstacles. Blessed are you who face the fire and are willing to walk through it. Blessed are you who receive My joy to overflowing. How the world needs you! How your brothers and sisters need you!

> Blessed are you who face the fire and are willing to walk through it.

Go out now, empowered in Who I am. Can your sight be more clear? Can it be more focused than it is now? Ah — yet so much more awaits you. But to get to the end, you have to make a beginning. Rejoice now, for you are only scratching the surface, My friend.

SCRIPTURE
"He who has the bride is the bridegroom; but the friend of the bridegroom, who stands and hears him, rejoices greatly because of the bridegroom's voice. Therefore this joy of mine is fulfilled." (John 3:29)

Further References: Psalm 51:1-8, 87:7; Isaiah 43:1-7; Jeremiah 33:10-11; Matthew 25:20-21; Hebrews 12:12

Let Me Heal Your Pain

When the pain comes on strong, you instinctively want to draw away. That is when I say, "Come near." Come near to Me, come near to one another, come near to the pain. Many of My people believe they have let go of their lives. They believe they have given Me control of their wills, their desires, their paths. But in reality, they still are holding on to a thousand different things.

The only way to true and perfect release is through the pain. You must die a thousand deaths along the way. Remember, your ability to deceive yourself is great. The way to true righteousness is through honesty and humility. I want to remove the veils, but you must come to Me so that I can do so. Why do you spend time in idle talk, daydreaming, or watching television, when all along, the gnawing pain inside continues to go unmet?

You can suppress the pain ... you can try to deny it ... you can attempt to escape it ... but it still remains. It may be loneliness, rejection, abandonment, fear, or shame. Let Me touch it so it will be no more. Let Me show you how futile your efforts are to deal with the pain. Let Me show you how My Spirit desires to be released among My people as a healer of their pain, not as a condemner, or a criticizer, or a taskmaster.

Come, My people, love one another in your pain. Let Me flow through you as vessels to heal the hurts you all carry. How can you walk in My perfect will with a perfect image of yourself, when this world has marred every child born within it? Come, My children, let Me heal you. Turn towards one another; receive one another in love. Let My love guide you. Let it lead you into all that I have called you to be.

Bow Down

You think you are doing nothing worthwhile. You think you are ineffective in My kingdom, and are not part of advancing My Light into this dark world. Oh, My child, can't you see that there is so much going on right now that doesn't have to do with what you see and do?

The words of your culture have to do with "effectiveness" and "productivity." Few speak of waiting for the Power from on high. Sure, you speak about the period of waiting for My answer, but do you really know what I desire to achieve during this time? Waiting requires a constant surrender of one's self. Waiting will carve out a humility within the heart that cannot be taken away. Waiting will usher in the total dependence upon Me that I desire within My loved ones.

I am interested in a soft, pliable heart that has been cultivated through periods of self-denial, barrenness, and silence. Those who are meek shall inherit the earth. I was meek, lowly, and humble. I carried not an ounce of pride.

Let Me carve within you My character, My child. Bow down to the pain and circumstances I have allowed in your life. Bow down to them as you would embrace My best gifts, because My best gifts are those worked within your heart. My best gifts are, in essence, more of Me. This is your highest purpose, this is your highest praise: to offer yourself as a vessel, a container, to be filled with more of Me.

> Let Me carve within you My character, My child.

Suffering in the Flesh

Jesus, Jesus why do we suffer so much in this life when we set upon a course to pursue You with all our heart? Right now I speak of suffering from emotional hurt, Lord — a deep, stabbing pain inflicted from a close friend by his words and action. I am bleeding, Lord; help me to understand.

My child, how well I know the pain you feel. The steps I walked in My three years were steps of pain, because I agonized over the condition of My Father's people. I was misunderstood by My very disciples; I was yelled at, conspired against, denied by one of My best friends, betrayed by another, and crucified on a cross.

> I ask you: Are you worthy of Me?
>
> Are you willing to accept your cross?

Any man or woman who follows Me — who TRULY seeks to follow Me — is asking Me to help them take the narrow road. He or she is asking Me for THE CROSS. My words are TRUTH, and they are HARD. "Anyone who does not take his cross and follow Me is not worthy of Me" (Matthew 10:38, NIV). I ask you: Are you worthy of Me? Are you willing to accept your cross?

Your hurt is real, and I promise to meet you there. From there, I will never leave you, because it is there that I can empower you. When you give up your right to be angry, to harden your heart, to want to strike back in vengeance, you are giving up your self. I made Myself nothing, and taking the nature of a servant, I humbled Myself in order to die. Now, I am exalted to the highest place. (Philippians 2:7-8).

I can be exalted in you only when you empty yourself. As you walk in My path, I am transforming you into My likeness. I will manifest Myself to you in your pain, and in your willingness to submit your pain to Me. As you are willing to submit your pain to Me, I will come forth out of you in ever-increasing glory.

I am in absolute control, My friend. The evil one can do no harm in this matter. He has lost, and you can confirm his defeat by allowing My sanctifying power to transform the very wound that's bleeding now into another scar of victory for My glory. Allow Me — I am here to do it.

SCRIPTURE
"But we all, with unveiled face, beholding as in a mirror the glory of the Lord, are being transformed into the same image from glory to glory, just as by the Spirit of the Lord". (2 Corinthians 3:18)

"Let this mind be in you which was also in Christ Jesus, who, being in the form of God, did not consider it robbery to be equal with God, but made Himself of no reputation, taking the form of a bondservant, and coming in the likeness of men. And being found in appearance as a man, He humbled Himself and became obedient to the point of death, even the death of the cross." (Philippians 2:5-8)

Further Reference: 2 Corinthians 4:11

Where Have You Been?

Where have you been? Where have you been? Don't you know that I want your love? You wonder why — why is it that you feel so dry? Could it be that in your zeal, you have gradually come to neglect Me?

If I am not first, if I am not your source, then what is it that propels you? You say it's your desire to serve Me, to meet the needs that are out there — and, yes, there are so many. But I ask you, What about your needs? What about my desires?"

I desire you to love Me. You need to love Me. This is your deepest need. It's why I came — to bridge the gap that sin brought between you and your Heavenly Father. Now you are trying to live as though I never came, yet you claim to be living for Me.

Do you know why I said that these were the two greatest commandments? Because I created you. I know your need.

It wasn't the grossest of sins that drove Adam and Eve out of the garden. You tend to look on killing as one of the worst offenses against Me. But no, the worst offenses against Me are the most civilized, the most easily hidden ones: selfish ambition and pride. There is something inherent in every human being that wants to live out his or her own course, while simultaneously giving lip service to Me.

Please, dear one, do not allow yourself to fall into that trap. Follow My two greatest commandments, and your well will not run dry. "The first of all the commandments is … Love the Lord your God with all your heart, with all your soul, with all your mind, and with all your strength. … And the second, like it, is this: You shall your neighbor as yourself. There is no other commandment greater than these." (Mark 12:29-31). Do you know why I said that these were the two greatest commandments? Because I created you. I know your need. I put it in you. You must love yourself correctly before you love others, and correct love for yourself follows only after you honor Me as your Way of Life, your Rescuer from Death, your Redeemer to Wholeness.

SCRIPTURE
"He who has My commandments and keeps them, it is he who loves Me. And he who loves Me will be loved by My Father, and I will love him and manifest Myself to him."
(John 14:21)

Can You Trust?

My words are true and they are right. I am faithful in all that I do. I love righteousness and justice. Let there be no deceit in your spirit. (Psalm 32:2). Let there be no pride in you. (Psalm 31:23).

Your hope must be in Me ALONE. Do you know how often I speak this ONE TRUTH throughout Scripture? Yet, it is so minimally grasped, even by My dearest followers. In so many ways, you take your path and your life back into your own hands; into your own insights, thoughts, and good ideas; into your own understanding. Why is it so hard to put your trust and your hope in Me and leave it there?

> Why is it so hard to put your trust and your hope in Me and leave it there?

"We wait in hope for our Lord; He is our help and our shield. In Him our hearts rejoice, for we trust in His holy name." (Psalm 33:20-21, NIV). Can you wait? Can you trust? Can your hearts rejoice in Me while you are waiting? Why is waiting so difficult? My principles go against this fast-paced culture in which you dwell. I promise that My unfailing love will rest upon those who put their hopes in Me. (Psalm 33:22). You have all the freedom (Psalm 32:10) to wander outside of the shelter of My presence (Psalm 31:20).

Don't you see? It is so simple. Those who dwell, who hope, who trust in Me, are promised the shelter of My unfailing love. I will never remove My love from you: rather, it is you who have the power to step outside the covering of love that I provide.

You Are Targeted

"There is therefore now no condemnation to those who are in Christ Jesus … for the law of the Spirit of life in Christ Jesus has made me free from the law of sin and death." (Romans 8:1-2).

[Again, I speak to you: You must know the power of the enemy; you must learn his tactics and his ability to cripple instantaneously. I have taught you much, yet I am teaching you more now.]

Do not underestimate his power and his drive. You are targeted. He will fight you on every front to discourage you and to get you to doubt My Spirit in you. Now, more than ever, you must not question who you are in Me, and Who I am in you. You must not question what you have heard from Me.

I am strengthening your inner man in ways you have never imagined.

Know this: if you wonder where I am or why you are allowed to feel so comfortless at times, it is because of My love for you. I am strengthening your inner man in ways you have never imagined. "I pray that out of His glorious riches He may strengthen you with power through His Spirit in your inner being." (Ephesians 3:16, NIV). I am teaching you to discern the enemy's voice, his presence, and his deception immediately, so you, in turn, will refute his tactics.

This is not a time to second-guess what I have taught you. You may not be fully aware of the comfort I bring, but I will assure you of My presence. It may come unexpectedly through the phone call of a believer or the smile of one who can be trusted. Take these to heart; they are My signposts along the way.

Fine Tuning

I am fine-tuning you. You are going to be an instrument of Mine that is razor-sharp. I spend much time pruning those of Mine who seek Me. Once I break them of their own strength, I begin to build them up in My strength. Many people will use the expression, "The Lord is my strength," when they are actually relying on their own resources. My strength is a mystery to many. I want to supply it, but many will fight the road which takes them there.

I must break you of your own strength; then I will build you up in Mine. But my transformation of you doesn't come overnight. It requires patience, humility, and a surrendered heart. While you are waiting for Me, you may be tempted to grab hold of something temporary, while I desire to give you only the eternal.

> My strength cannot be viewed apart from an understanding of My grace.

Not everything that looks good, feels good, or sounds good is the way to My best. I am waiting to give My best, but I do require you to wait on Me. If you are content with what comes by way of nature, or even giftedness, that is where I will leave you. But if you want My strength, it must be imparted by My grace. It doesn't come naturally, and you can't earn it. If you desire My strength, allow Me to take you to a place of need and then wait for it. It's free to those that need it and wait for it. My strength has to do with grace. My strength cannot be viewed apart from an understanding of My grace.

SCRIPTURE

"'Now see that I, even I, am He, And there is no God besides Me; I kill and I make alive; I wound and I heal; Nor is there any who can deliver from My hand." (Deuteronomy 32:39)

"Behold, I will make you into a new threshing sledge with sharp teeth; you shall thresh the mountains and beat them small, and make the hills like chaff. You shall winnow them, the wind shall carry them away, and the whirlwind shall scatter them; you shall rejoice in the Lord, and glory in the Holy One of Israel." (Isaiah 41:15-16)

"And lest I should be exalted above measure by the abundance of the revelations, a thorn in the flesh was given to me, a messenger of Satan to buffet me, lest I be exalted above measure. Concerning this thing I pleaded with the Lord three times that it might depart from me. And He said to me, 'My grace is sufficient for you, for My strength is made perfect in weakness.' Therefore most gladly I will rather boast in my infirmities, that the power of Christ may rest upon me. Therefore I take pleasure in infirmities, in reproaches, in needs, in persecutions, in distresses, for Christ's sake. For when I am weak, then I am strong." (2 Corinthians 12:7-10)

Further References: 1 Samuel 2:1-10; Isaiah 40:31, 66:1; Psalm 37:4-11, Ezekiel 37:1-14; 2 Corinthians 4:16-18; Hebrews 6:15, 12:5-11; 1 Peter 5:6

Learn My Way of Love

You ask Me why it is so hard. You wonder why you are asked to die so many times, through one trial after another. Why so many altars of sacrifice, so many crosses of sorrow and suffering.

Hear Me when I say to you, My friend, that I am not abandoning you during your pain. It would be much worse if I left you alone to your flesh. I see your heart; it de sires to have as much of Me as you can in this life. Having more of Me means walking My path and embracing My cross daily.

I know too well the pain of walking in a sin-laden world. I came to save a lost world; but remember, you still exist within it. One day, there will be no more pain, no more sorrow, no more suffering. But until then, I will use these as tools to draw you into communion with Me.

> An army without Love will quickly be devoured by itself.

I can only use those who readily lay down their lives. It is painful to die, but the more you do, the more I can live in you. Don't dwell on the dying; dwell on the purpose behind it. That purpose is Love. One day you won't live in your frail fleshly nature; instead, you will see Me as I am, and you will know how priceless your trials are.

Love is a force that My church knows little about right now. Love has little to do with feelings, but it has much to do with power. In your flesh, you cannot love. Your flesh strains against love, because selfishness cannot come near Love. Love has to do with emptying oneself.

But how many of My people live like this? You must seek to learn this way of Love. An army without Love will quickly be devoured by itself. Love dies over and over — so it can expand. Too many seek to hold onto their lives and they quench Love.

But also realize that those who try to die on their own terms — those who pick and choose where they will die — are often those who miss My voice. Often times, the way I am asking you to die will be the most painful, and, unlike many "good works" for My kingdom, your death may not be visible to others. An obvious sacrifice is usually not the one I will call you to. My call to sacrifice is a matter of the heart. That is why there is no way to measure it on the earth. This is the Love that will allow My army to function in perfect unity. There will be no comparing oneself to another, for your success will only fully be revealed in eternity.

SCRIPTURE
"This is My commandment, that you love one another as I have loved you. Greater love has no one than this, than to lay down one's life for his friends." (John 15:12-13)

Further References: Psalm 51:17; Ephesians 3:16-19; Philippians 1:9-11, 2:5-11

Formidable Foe

Oh, afflicted and storm-tossed one! I will not leave you comfortless for long. I will build you into a beautiful living stone, one that shines with the light of My glory. There is no way you can fathom the plans I hold for eternity, for I am the Repairer of the Breach and I will come soon to take back what is rightfully Mine. I must have those with sturdy legs to carry My judgments, and I must have those with hearts of love that know no fear.

Great suffering induces one to panic, to fight back, to give in and to give up. But those who endure great suffering for no reason other than divine decree will find the capacity of their hearts enlarged to receive Me. Remember, you were called to suffer for doing good. I left you this example, and I have declared this to be the only way you may follow in My steps.

Great suffering induces one to panic.

The hordes of hell can do nothing to the saint who is completely aligned with my Father's will. There is no battle to be fought, because the battle begins over conquest of one's self. If you have allowed Me to completely conquer you, then you are fully Mine. You are viewed in the spiritual realm with fear and trembling, for though you may be outwardly broken and bruised, it is your submission to me that makes you such a formidable foe.

SCRIPTURE
"You also, as living stones, are being built up a spiritual house, a holy priesthood, to offer up spiritual sacrifices acceptable to God through Jesus Christ ... For this is commendable, if because of conscience toward God one endures grief, suffering wrongfully. For what credit is it if, when you are beaten for your faults, you take

it patiently? But when you do good and suffer, if you take it patiently, this is commendable before God. For to this you were called, because Christ also suffered for us, leaving us an example, that you should follow His steps: 'Who committed no sin, nor was deceit found in His mouth'; Who, when He was reviled, did not revile in return; when He suffered, He did not threaten, but committed Himself to Him who judges righteously." (1 Peter 2:5, 19-23)

Further References: Psalm 12:5-6; Isaiah 54:11-17

An Undivided Heart

"I will give them an undivided heart and put a new spirit in them; I will remove from them their heart of stone and give them a heart of flesh." (Ezekiel 11:19, NIV)

Deep down in your heart you must be undivided. Being unified with Me brings unity within yourself and then to the rest of My body. You must know who you are. Before you are released into "who you are," you must know "who you are." The vision must be deep down inside of you, given my Me. You must see it and walk in it in your heart first. Therefore, your identity is never and will never be determined or affirmed by external realities.

Remember also that to be united with Me requires total transparency on your part. An undivided heart is pure, clean, and truthful. It becomes undivided through the purification of all falsehood.

SCRIPTURES
"Teach me your way, O LORD, and I will walk in your truth; give me an undivided heart, that I may fear your name." (Psalm 86:11, NIV)

"I will sprinkle clean water on you, and you will clean; I will cleanse you from all your impurities and from all your idols." (Ezekiel 36:25, NIV)

Further References: 2 Corinthians 3:3; Psalm 24:3-4; Ezekiel 4:21-25, 36:25-28

The Revelation of My Love

It is the revelation of My love that casts out all fear, all discouragement, all hopelessness. It is not self-effort, or what many refer to as the "battle of the mind" or spiritual warfare. Spiritual warfare is a reality, but the strength of one's warfare is dependent upon the foundation of love within him or her. Many people fight all day long, "waging warfare" when My love desires to set them free. All fleshly works and self-effort will fall away during the last days. The only thing that will stand is what is built upon My love. The power of evil will stand tall, but the power of My love will stand taller. Anything in between will fall.

Yes, the lie of self-effort has been taught in My church. The only ones who will stand in the days ahead are those who have not lived according to this lie, but have been set free by My love. Only perfect love casts out all fear; anything else will fail.

I am trying to perfect My lovers with My perfect love. But the lie that says you are here first and foremost to fight must be dismantled. You are here first and foremost to love. Only this will stand. Only this will last.

"Warfare" is done in love. "Warfare" is realizing that I have already won the war, and you are called to stand and advance in My victory. But you will only stand by My love.

SCRIPTURE
"It is the Spirit who gives life; the flesh profits nothing. The words that I speak to you are spirit, and they are life." (John 6:63). "There is no fear in love; but perfect love casts out fear, because fear involves punishment. Be he who fears has not been made perfect in love." (1 John 4:18)

Dwell Upon Me

You are in My hands, My child. The constant pressure and intense stress you feel is meant to purify you of what is still lurking in your carnal nature. Your focus must be on Me. I am even purifying your gaze so that through eyes of purity you will see that I am all you need. Your eyes upon Me must remain steadfast and unwavering.

My glory resides within you, but it is enshrouded within a human covering. To see Me, your flesh must not be in the way. In order to bring your will into alignment with Mine, you must dwell upon Me. Cease striving and be still. The flesh strives; it sees imperfection and strives to make things right.

To see Me, your flesh must not be in the way.

But your spirit sees perfection as its gazes upon Me. I have no blemish. I am perfect goodness, and perfect in loveliness. But if you hadn't been brought to such a point of desperation, do you think you would have seen Me as such? Yet, in all eternity, this is how you will see Me — perfect. Spend much time dwelling upon Me as infinite beauty and absolute perfection. Doing so here in this life will prepare you for Me in eternity.

SCRIPTURE

"Beloved, now we are children of God; and it has not yet been revealed what we shall be, but we know that when He is revealed, we shall be like Him, for we shall see Him as He is. And everyone who has this hope in Him purifies himself, just as He is pure." (1 John 3:2-3)

Further References: Psalm 46:10; 2 Corinthians 3:16-18.

Perfect Submission

Seek not after peace. Seek not after "good things." Seek only perfect submission to My will. But perfect submission does not come overnight. It only comes after much pain and many dealings with your "self." And, it only comes by the power of My Holy Spirit.

Ask and you will receive. But remember, I learned obedience through suffering. If you have asked for a submissive will, then expect suffering. If you have asked for more faith, it will be given you, but it will not be handed to you upon a silver platter. You will be taken into experiences where you are pressed beyond measure and where you feel there is no way to walk through. This is where faith is born.

Like a lamb led to slaughter.

When I was upon the cross, I did not verbally rebuke the enemy. "Like a lamb led to slaughter," I did not open My mouth. Those who are meek shall inherit the earth.

When you are upon the cross, you must silently bear the wrongs. Ask Me for the grace to do it. Upon the cross, you may experience mental and emotional exhaustion. My enemy will jump upon this opportunity to badger you. But remember, I did not fight back. My friend, just die with Me.

SCRIPTURE
"He was oppressed and He was afflicted, Yet He opened not His mouth; He was led as a lamb to the slaughter, And as a sheep before its shearers is silent, So He opened not His mouth." (Isaiah 53:7)

Further References: Matthew 16:23, 26:36-42; Luke 22:42-44; John 12:26-27; Hebrews 5:7-8

Submitting to My Lordship

Who can proclaim Me as Lord? Only those who know Me as Lord — through and through. Today I long to possess you in all ways. Today you must ask Me how it is I desire you to submit to My Lordship. As I submitted to the Roman authorities by carrying My cross through the city, you too can pick up your cross today by asking Me how it is I am calling you to submit to My Lordship.

Many of My followers become stuck in their routine of how they submit to My Lordship. But I am always creating new ways for My loved ones to pick up their crosses daily. To those who venture in faith to ask Me, and have the boldness to step out of comfort zones, the cross becomes a joy … the joy of all the endless ways of discovering My Lordship … the joy of all the ways of proclaiming Me by receiving My daily offer of embracing the cross … the joy of deeper communion with Me in My death, so that My life may be more completely released within you.

> But I am always creating new ways for My loved ones to pick up their crosses daily.

SCRIPTURE

"As the Father loved Me, I also have loved you; abide in My love. If you keep My commandments, you will abide in My love, just as I have kept My Father's commandments and abide in His love. These things I have spoken to you, that My joy may remain in you, and that your joy may be full. This is My commandment, that you love one another as I have loved you. Greater love has no one than this, than to lay down one's life for his friends. You are My friends if you do whatever I command you." (John 15:9-14)

"So that they may have the full measure of My joy within them." (John 17:13)

I Am Still on the Throne

I am still on the throne, My friend. Never forget this. When everything — literally, everything — seems to contradict this, you must know that this is true. Allow it to become cemented into every fiber of your being. I am still on the throne. I am still on the throne. I have not stepped off for a second; no, I have not even glanced away from you. You are always in My thoughts; My eyes are always upon you.

I am still on the throne

Many may fail you. You may become disillusioned by friends; indeed, by My very body. This is the time you must dwell upon this Truth and speak it over and over as water to your soul, until My peace reigns. I am still on the throne.

SCRIPTURE
Further References: Psalm 3, 10:17-18, 27, 33:13-18.

Access His Power

Even if you have only 1% left of your strength (body, mind, emotions), your faith in my power within you can move you further along than I you had 99% of you strength intact.

Your weakness accesses My power.

Remember this, dwell upon it and allow it to take you from glory to glory. It is the Divine Mystery. I emptied myself and became man. When you are empty, I will become your strength. All you will need is faith the size of a mustard seed. You don't need to feel strong. You don't need to feel faithful. All you need to do is believe, and I am there!

Love in Action

Lord, I know that, "if I have all the knowledge in the world, but I have not love, then I am nothing" (1 Corinthians 13:2, NIV).

I want to satisfy you with My love, but before I can do so, you must come to the point where you are truly satisfied only with Me. When this is present, then you can fulfill My command in (Matthew 6:33 NIV): "But seek first His kingdom and His righteousness, and all these things will be given to you as well."

Remember, it is much easier to say that you love than to meet the demands of love. However, My command to love is much simpler and more straightforward than My people have made it. This is love in action — simple obedience, with purpose and without complaint. The world is to know Me by the love you have for one another. It may be easier for some of you to love from afar, to say that you love the lost, but not be obedient to love those directly in front of you. I will show you who you are to love and how you are to love them, and I will give you the strength to do so.

SCRIPTURE
"He who has My commandments and keeps them, it is he who loves Me. And he who loves Me will be loved by My Father, and I will love him and reveal Myself to him." (John 14:21)

"Beloved, if God so loved us, we also ought to love one another. No one has seen God at any time. If we love one another, God abides in us, and His love has been perfected in us." (1 John 4:11-12)

Further references: Matthew 5:43-48; John 13:12-17, 34-35; Colossians 3:14; 1 John 3:16-21

Above All … Love

Keep love at the forefront. No matter what happens, love. When you are hurt, love. When you are misunderstood, love. When you are neglected, love. When you are ridiculed, love. This simple word, when lived out to its fullest, has the power to change the universe.

Love is the ultimate reason you were created. I am always offering you doors to deeper love, avenues to deeper joy, pathways to deeper peace. You must seek these opportunities.

In the life of every individual I created, I have placed open doors. It is up to you to walk through these doors. Oftentimes the door itself will appear uninviting, but My true lovers will always be obedient to walk through, and they will go deeper and deeper into Me.

But even for those who do not know me, My love knows no bounds. Can you imagine what it would be like to experience the depths of My love for my whole creation? Imagine the depths of My love for you, and add to it the billions of people I have created throughout time. If you tilted your head back, could you receive even one drop? And yet, I am longing to pour it out. Can you receive it? Will you be willing to expand your container, so I can pour it out upon you and among you?

SCRIPTURE

"As the Father loved Me, I also have loved you; abide in My love. If you keep My commandments, you will abide in My love, just as I have kept My Father's commandments and abide in His love. These things I have spoken to you, that My joy may remain in you, and that your joy may be full." (John 15:9-11)

Further References: Ephesians 3:16-20; 1 Corinthians 13:1-13; I Peter 4:8.

Come Capture Me

Every day, you have the choice of whether or not you will spend it with Me.

Some interruptions are by My Hand. But many disturbances are exactly that — disturbances. You will see them as they truly are only if your focus is streamlined upon Me. I am the One who will clean the lens of your eyes. I am the One who will enable you to see clearly. My beloved one, come capture Me, and you will be captured. Come behold Me, and you will be held by My gaze.

Many are the enemies of such romance. But once captured, you shall be forever held. This is My promise and assurance as you go out behind the enemy lines. I am the seal upon your heart.

> Come behold Me, and you will be held by My gaze.

SCRIPTURE
"Place me like a seal over your heart, like a seal on your arm; for love is as strong as death, its jealousy unyielding as the grave. It burns like blazing fire, like a mighty flame." (Song of Solomon 8:6, NIV)

"The lamp of the body is the eye. If therefore your eye is good, your whole body will be full of light. But if your eye is bad, your whole body will be full of darkness. If therefore the light that is in you is darkness, how great is that darkness!" (Matthew 6:22-23)

Purity

In order to lead My people to freedom, your heart must be completely transformed by My love. There must not be an ounce of pride, judgment, or superiority. In the Spirit realm, these hindrances, no matter how small they may seem, become great obstacles to the release of My power. Your enemy can only be dismantled through purity, for he will attach himself to any snag within your heart and mind. This is why My training is intended to produce pure hearts. Only those with pure hearts will be able to march unharmed through the enemy's strongholds. Only those with clean hands will gain the respect necessary to ignite the hunger in people's hearts for true freedom.

> Your enemy can only be dismantled through PURITY.

SCRIPTURE
Further References: Psalm 24:4, 51:10-17; Ezekiel 11:19-20; Matthew 7:1-5, 7:20-23, 12:34-37.

New Wine

The river of unrest you feel is not always from the enemy. I am stirring My people to greater heights of obedience and perfection. As I have said, "The old wineskins will burst when the new wine is poured in."

My new wine is ready to be poured, but I am in the process of preparing My container to receive it. Within your self, within your relationships, within your body of believers, there is a stirring, a discontentment. I ask you, who can be content in what is not yet in its purest form?

> I am preparing you to receive more.

My people must be free from all manipulation and control, all falsehood, all pride and jealousy. Every word spoken and every action carried out must be done unto Me. Preparation for the new wine is uncomfortable to your outer nature, but freeing to your spirit. Because your spirit hungers for more, I am preparing you to receive more. Those who do not resist the change will receive the new life I am waiting to pour out.

"Unconditional" Desires

You were birthed into a world of expectations.
But I have no expectations of you.
I have only many desires for you, and those desires are not conditioned upon your performance, or even your response to Me. You may turn your back, you may reject My counsel, you may keep yourself too busy for Me — but I will keep on loving you.

Messengers of Truth

Do not be dismayed by the darkness covering the earth. You must be able to look at the darkness with the hope of My glory rising in your heart.

Many do not know Me. That is why I call you to enter into the darkness and lead them out. All they see and sense is the darkness, and they will take any path that they presume will lead them out. That is why you must show them the true path. The enemy has many deceptions that shine like light, but lead to greater darkness. Any path outside of My cross is a path of deception.

My path is actually quite simple. This is why those who perceive themselves to be intelligent will have difficulty finding it. They view the world through their minds, and they have erected a barrier around their hearts. But I find My entrance though the heart. I created every heart to be in union with Me, and every one will be restless until they rest in Me. You must go out and find those restless hearts and lead them to Me.

> Any path outside of My cross is a path of deception.

Anyone who seeks freedom through the mind will indeed receive a way out, but it is a way into greater deception. You must be messengers of truth, even while the author of deception has his own messengers. You must speak for the truth, and remove the veil of deception. Remember, deception is effective because it is attractive to the mind's eye. Through the power of My word, you must remove the blinders of those who are deceived. You must go forth as I send you.

Basking In Me

Repent. Rest. Be quiet. Trust.
Repent. Rest. Be quiet. Trust.

"For thus says the Lord God, the Holy One of Israel: 'In returning and rest you shall be saved; in quietness and confidence shall be your strength." (Isaiah 30:15).

What would you do without the sunshine? What would you do without its warmth? Look around you. Really take a look, and see My beauty in all its fullness. Let it lead you to reverence; let it lead you to worship. It is my gift to you, a mere glimpse of all I have in store. Drink it in. Allow yourself to be filled through and through with the beauty of Who I am. Where words cannot touch, breathe it in.

> Allow yourself to be filled through and through with the beauty of Who I am.

I am your life source. There are days to work, but to advance in effort and growth, you must set aside days such as these ... to bask in Me ... to dig your roots down deep ... and to be filled without measure with all My fullness. (Ephesians 3:19).

Preparation

Pour your hearts out before Me, My chosen ones (Psalm 62:8). Pour them out like water. Pour out all of your life, all of your cares. Truly, many can say that they have been crucified with Me, but crucifixion does not occur overnight. There is preparation that is painful, slow, and laborious, but its purpose is to enable you to embrace the cross.

> You cannot live *for* Me, you can only live *in* Me.

You must hold nothing dear to you, My friends — nothing except My will. In My will is your freedom. Walking in My will is your sustenance. Many of My people claim to be living for Me, yet they are starving. You cannot live *for* Me, you can only live *in* Me. And to do this, you must be crucified. Ask Me if you are truly willing to die for Me.

I must show many people what holds them back. If you could see through spiritual eyes the life My resurrection power brings, you would lay everything down and come to Me.

Come to Me while there is still time. Come to Me, and allow Me to live My life in and through you.

Come to Me, know what the real meaning of love is, and walk in that love for My people.

SCRIPTURE
Further References: John 4:34, 5:30, 6:38, 8:29, 15:4-5, 7-10; Galatians 2:20.

The Way of Faith

Behold, I am making all things new. It is My Word alone that spoke you into being. It is My Word alone that will bring all things to pass.

And you must feed upon My Word alone. You must never take your eyes off of Me. When you do, My Word cannot hold you. There is a test going on right now. What will you choose to live by? What or who will you look to for guidance? Will you find your food in doing My will? Or will you look to other methods to "supplement" you?

I am teaching you the way of faith. Not faith in what you are, what you can do, or what you see around you, but faith in Me alone. You must walk onto the sea without anything to hold on to. I cannot be your life if you still carry the world's life preservers. You may want to put me to the test, but I have already passed all your tests. Just believe. It is as simple as this. Just believe.

You must walk onto the sea without ANYTHING to hold on to.

SCRIPTURE
"Ignoring what they said, Jesus told the synagogue ruler, 'Don't be afraid; just believe.'"
(Mark 5:36)

Further References: Matthew 4:3-10, 8:5-10, 14:27-31; John 6:63, 14:1.

Your Mind Must Be Renewed

Your youth will return in the measure that you have cast off all yokes that are not Mine. What does it mean, "I run in the freedom of Your commands"? I created you to run, not to stand still. Yet many of My runners are barely moving; many have dropped out because of burnout. Weariness comes when My runners are carrying yokes they are not intended to carry. Only through deep intimacy with Me will you see clearly which yokes you have picked up that are not Mine. My love is always reaching out, pouring out to you. But the lies within your mind distort both the reality of My presence and the clarity of My voice.

> But the lies within your mind distort both the reality of My presence and the clarity of My voice.

Your ability to receive Me depends on how much your mind has been renewed. My commands are not burdensome. The lies are what oppress you and open the door to the enemy. Come, let Me disclose the lies and replace them with the truth. Watch your life and your "running" closely, and be transformed by the miracle of My love.

SCRIPTURE
"And you shall know the truth, and the truth shall make you free." (John 8:32)

"I beseech you therefore, brethren, by the mercies of God, that you present your bodies a living sacrifice, holy, acceptable to God, which is your reasonable service. And do not be conformed to this world, but be transformed by the renewing of your mind, that you may prove what is that good and acceptable and perfect will of God." (Romans 12:1-2)

Who You Are

I never send you out unprepared. Everything I call you to do, I equip you to do. First you are called … then you are chosen … then you are prepared. I will commission you, once I determine that your preparation is complete.

It is a tactic of the enemy — and a weakness of the flesh — to push you into your calling before My commissioning. This is why you must first be healed of all insecurities. Otherwise, you will rush into your commissioning, because it gives you identity. All of My chosen ones know their identity comes from Me alone, but they don't "know" it deep in their heart. It must reside there in order to complete My protection from the enemy's tactics. Therefore, much of the preparation time is intended to bring about a deep revelation of "who you are" in Me. And "who you are" is far deeper than "what you do" for Me.

Who you are is far deeper than *what you do* for Me.

Union With Another

The secret to all relationships is this: dwell in Me. Remember, I am the opposite of all strife, and only in Me will My loved ones be established in love. Enter all relationships with the desire to seek the best for Me, not with the question of "What can I get out of this?" Relationships are a main avenue I use in order to bring death to your selfishness. I must kill within each of My children the inherent drive that says, "What can I get out of this?" and replace it with, "What does my Lord desire to do with this relationship?"

Union occurs when there is TRUST. Your trust in Me must be wholehearted.

I desire for relationships to bring about union with one another. Many of My people have shied away from one another because of the focus on dysfunctional relationships and their distinctive nature. Such revelation was never meant to drive people apart; its purpose is to reveal enemy strongholds and dismantle them. But in many ways, My people have taken the world's approach to dysfunction and allowed individualism to become their guide.

I have instructed you to guard your heart, because within it lies the wellspring of life. But you must learn to "unguard" it as well, as I determine it safe for you to do so. Union with Me (or union with one another) cannot occur with walls of protection, because the walls only serve to insulate fear. Union occurs when there is trust.

Your trust in Me must be wholehearted. Then you can abandon yourself in trust with one another.

Your heart must be young, supple, pliable, joyful to accomplish these unions. It cannot be full of suspicion, hurt, and mistrust. Much hardness of heart exists within My followers. Even those who are sincere have been wounded, and their hearts are heavily guarded. Pray for My softening to come.

SCRIPTURE
"I do not pray for these alone, but also for those who will believe in Me through their word; that they all may be one, as You, Father, are in Me, and I in You; that they also may be one in Us, that the world may believe that You sent Me. And the glory which You gave Me I have given them, that they may be one just as We are one: I in them and You in Me; that they may be made perfect in one, and that the world may know that You have sent Me, and have loved them as You have loved Me". (John 17:20-23)

Further Reference: 1 John 4:15-21.

New You

Truly, you must arrive at the place where, should all the world turn against you, you would be able to stand alone because of your confidence in Me, in you. The answer is not outward, it is within. This is what you have asked for and this is what you will receive, but it can only be received by you. It is given by Me, but must be received by you.

Do you understand? You must take a step to receive it. It is a whole new identity that is awaiting you. A whole new you … made complete by Me.

Freedom is Coming

There is a great and marvelous freedom coming to My body, a freedom that is received to the degree that the truth is embraced. If your heart seeks freedom, you must be ready to see the truth. Freedom comes to those who worship in Spirit and in truth. No matter how much you may seek to walk in My Spirit and worship Me in Spirit, if you reject the truth in any measure — the truth about yourself, your character, your maturity, your world — you will be hindered.

My Spirit seeks truth, settles upon truth, and dwells in truth. In order for My people to grow into maturity, everyone must recognize where he or she is yet immature. Ah, such truth can be painful! But the truth is only painful to the extent that pride is operating in your life. Seek to uncover all areas of pride, and soon you will be one who not only welcomes the truth, but runs toward it. Those who run in that freedom are the ones who will share in My delight as they advance rapidly toward the goal and do not fall behind My Spirit.

The wind of My Spirit blows where it wills. You do not know where it comes from or where it is going, but you will always be in step with it as you dwell in truth. My Spirit cannot dwell in any falsehood. So, I ask you: do you want to move in the great freedom that is coming?

SCRIPTURE
"Yet a time is coming, and has now come, when the true worshippers will worship the Father in Spirit and truth, for they are the kind of worshippers the Father seeks. God is Spirit, and His worshippers must worship in Spirit and truth." (John 4:23-24, NIV)

"I run in the path of Your commands, for You have set my heart free." (Psalm 119:32, NIV)

Further References: John 15:26, 16:13, 17:17

True Strength

There is a weakness that is really a strength, and there is a strength that is really a weakness. Many who appear to be strong are actually very weak. Many who seem to be weak and frail are actually living upon the strength that is true.

> Many times, strength is a stubborn refusal to let go and die.

I do not call you to walk by the vision of this world. I call you to walk by faith. Many, many times your outer man must be brought to the point of crumbling, in order for you to know what strength really is. My power comes in at the point of utter powerlessness. Many of My people declare this from their mouth, but do not truly live it from their heart. How blessed it is to be able to say, "I cannot go on … I want Your way, not mine."

As a child I call you. (Matthew 18:3). Do not be deceived by those who appear to be strong. Many times, strength is a stubborn refusal to let go and die. Those who are mature in the faith must be mature enough to become like a child. Many are too proud and too wise in their own eyes to humble themselves like a child. Please accept My invitation. Learn weakness — and know My strength.

SCRIPTURE
Further References: Matthew 23:11-13; 1 Corinthians 1:23-29, 2:1-8; 2 Corinthians 12:9

Brave Hearts

You will always be tempted to depend upon your own strengths. You will always hold a measure of security in certain relationships. None of these are sinful, but there comes a point when I will decide to remove them — one at a time, perhaps, or all at once, pulling out all of your props, leaving you alone with all of your weaknesses laid bare.

> In Me, you can do all things that I have in My mind for you.

How heartless this seems of Me, but actually, it is My great mercy that leaves you in such a helpless state, naked and poor, broken and alone. Apart from Me, you can do nothing. In Me, you can do all things that I have in My mind for you.

How do you come to rely upon Me and Me alone? I am the Way, My child; I will perform this process in your life, if you deeply desire it in your inmost being. I alone search the hearts and minds of men, and I know those who speak words of dependency, but have little desire to live them. They rely far too much on outer things — their own strength, their own wisdom, their own external securities.

Then there are My children who deeply desire only Me as their strength. They seek total and absolute dependence upon Me, with nothing standing in the way. How I delight in such surrender! Immediately, I begin the process of bringing each one of these children into a state of radical dependency. Things you didn't know that you relied upon are suddenly removed. Personal strengths and graces you took for granted are all of a sudden gone.

When the last prop is removed, do not be afraid to fall. There is only one place you can fall now — deeper into Me. This is the only way to be dependent — desperately, radically dependent — upon Me. I will not have you declare that I am your strength, that I am your all in all, when you have many hidden props. As the process begins, remain in My love, for this will take a Brave Heart.

The Narrow Road
The path is straight, but it is also narrow. I made it that way so that the only way to reach Me is through single-mindedness. I made it that way so that My true followers would be separated from those who are not true.

You must purposefully turn off the voices of the world, the flesh, and the enemy. Remember, he would not be so successful if he were not a master of disguise and deception. He will come in through your friends, your fellow believers, or even your spouse. Usually he will dangle a carrot in front of you and say, "You'll get there more easily if you just veer off here, to the left a little." However, a tiny deviation from the straight and narrow now will result in a significant split down the road. You must realize that the further you grow in intimacy with Me, the narrower the road becomes.

> The further you grow in intimacy with Me, the narrower the road becomes.

SCRIPTURE
"From everyone who has been given much, much will be demanded; and from the one who has been entrusted with much, much more will be asked." (Luke 12:48, NIV)

Redemptive Love

There are many emotions of My Father's heart, and one of these is grief — grief for a world lost to the power of sin; grief for people in bondage to the reign of evil; grief for a body torn apart through the lack of understanding; grief for My children enslaved by the deceptions of the enemy; grief about such frail love exercised by My people. You were created for love, yet you are so unable to walk in it — as of yet.

Love in its truest, purest form is a force unstoppable. Love is redemptive. How many of you love in a way that redeems the object of your love? "Greater love has no one than this, that he lay down his life for his friends." John 15:13. There is a laying down of one's life that releases love, My Father's love, a love that sacrifices all for the sake of the other — all selfish desire, all simple desires, all logical reasoning. Can you love beyond logic? My cross makes no sense to the logical mind. It is an impossibility that I, God, came in human form and died for you to set you free. Free, not only from sin, but free from yourself and free from the world you live in.

Are you willing to receive My redemptive love? Be careful now in your answer, for if you say, "Yes!" you are going to be delivered from many of the ways you have learned to love. You are going to be grieved by what grieves my Father's heart, and your heart is going to be changed in the process. And, you are going to love others in a way that changes their hearts. This is redemptive love … a love that releases My love … a love beyond logic … a love free from self or self-gain … a love that will likely cost you great pain to keep on loving.

I am the source of this love, and the end of this love is Me. In between is a vessel who has rendered itself totally pliable in the hand of its Greatest Lover. Will you say "Yes!"?

A Spacious Place

"You have not handed me over to the enemy, but have set my feet in a spacious place." (Psalm 31:8, NIV).

Did you know that once I have set your feet in a spacious place, you have the freedom to step out? I created you to seek Me and to love Me with all your heart. If you are constantly seeking Me, you will dwell within My shelter. "He who dwells in the shelter of the Most High will rest in the shadow of the Almighty." I will not compete with the voices of the world that are set up to lure you away from Me as your center, your focus, your fortress. Even the Church will contain mixed voices — spirit and flesh thrown in together. You must always discern who is speaking.

I am the Lord, and there is no other. I make known the end from the beginning. I say, "My purpose will stand and I will do all that I please." Just as you are not to doubt Me, you are not to doubt My Spirit within you. What you hear in the quiet place — the deepest recesses of your heart — no one can touch that. Shut out the voices of loved ones, even those closest to you. I alone have the power to move you from one point to the next. You must allow yourself time to dwell with Me.

You must allow yourself time to dwell with Me.

SCRIPTURE
Further References: Isaiah 14:24, 27; 46:9-11

My View of You

I told you before, and I will tell you again: you must see yourself as I see you. I see you as My beloved friend, created to rule and reign with Me, indwelt with My invincible power. I am not saying you should puff yourself up in a false or prideful manner. But I am saying that you must seek to have My view of you and My vision of how you are to be in eternity! One day you will be perfect. One day you will be all-knowing, all-loving, without a single blemish. One day …

What if you could receive this truth for today and allow it to empower you for the tasks ahead? Your circumstances may seem overwhelming, and your own fleshly nature may cry out in frustration, in pain, in its true state of corruption. Advance with all knowledge that this will pass away, and what is born of the Spirit will last.

> In order to love truly and completely, you must know yourself as one who is deeply loved.

Many of the struggles My people have are mere distractions. There are real battles to be fought, but not until My people have a clear view of how I see them. This is why I am calling you to have My vision.

You must see yourself as I see you, and walk in the certainty of this Truth. You must see the people around you as I see them, and walk in the certainty of My love for them. If you have difficulty seeing My pure and perfect view of you, ask Me to show you. If the vision begins to slip away amidst trying circumstances, run to Me immediately and My Spirit will arise to renew your vision.

A true visionary can only proceed from the power of love. In order to love truly and completely, you must know yourself as one who is deeply loved. I have called all of My people to be visionaries; I have urged you to set your minds and hearts upon heavenly things, where I am seated at the right hand of My Father. Steady your gaze now. My will longs to come down from heaven. Do you long to receive it?

SCRIPTURE
"And do not be conformed to this world, but be transformed by the renewing of your mind, that you may prove what is that good and acceptable and perfect will of God." (Romans 12:2)

"Beloved, now we are children of God; and it has not yet been revealed what we shall be, but we know that when He is revealed, we shall be like Him, for we shall see Him as He is. And everyone who has this hope in Him purifies himself, just as He is pure." (1 John 3:2-3)

I Believe

Many of my people stand in their circumstances and look up toward Me. Their eyes are fixed upon Me and this is good. But what if you could view your circumstances from My perspective, from my realm of glory, looking into your earthly existence? Could you believe in miracles? Could you believe in my love? Come up higher, my child. Receive my view of your circumstances. Seek the revelation that transforms your heart and shifts your entire being. Go from dwelling in your self to dwelling in me.

SCRIPTURE
"For you have died and your life is hidden with Christ in God. When Christ, who is our life, is revealed, then you also will be revealed with Him in glory." (Colossians 3:3-4 NAS)

Run in Order to Win

I cannot emphasize how much less your mouth needs to be open and your mind needs to be thinking, and how much more your ears need to be open and your eyes need to be watching.

I am always speaking My directives, My words of assurance, My words of caution. You must realize that your greatest hindrance is yourself. You know this in your head, but to receive it in your heart, your wellspring of life, you must undergo great discipline, and one of your greatest blessings will be to receive this discipline from My hand. All that I allow within your circumstances will serve to teach you this way of life. You must know the disciplined life of one who walks in continual repentance and forgiveness. My love is waiting to cleanse you as you obediently put off your self-life. Too many of My children hide from Me in shame over their sin; or, in pride, they attempt to cover it up. As if you could hide either yourself or your sin from Me!

If only you could grasp the height and depth of My love for you! If you only knew how much I was for you, you would run to the cross! Who would not want the cleansing and refreshing that comes from My blood? How can you be ashamed of something you inherited? You were born into original sin. You didn't cause it, but you can participate on its behalf. If you say you are without sin, you deceive yourself. You must have a sober view of yourself. You were created in My image, yet your nature is steeped in sin. My Spirit will lift you out according to your discipline in seeking Me. Those who walk the narrow road do so with discipline and determination. Many runners run the race, but not everyone runs to win. You must run in order to win.

SCRIPTURE
Further References: Proverbs 20:9; Matthew 12:36-37; 1 Corinthians 9:24-27; 1 John 1:8-10

Am I Your Life?

In Me, you'll find fullness, and joy, and contentment. Outside of Me, you'll find strife, discontent, and pain.

It is not about your circumstances, or what is going on in your life. It is all about your dwelling. Are you dwelling in Me, or are you dwelling in your "self?" If you are dwelling in your "self," you are tearing at the very essence of your purpose. You see, you were created to abide in Me and to be of one mind with Me. But your "self" will pull against its only true fulfillment. Your jar of clay will instinctively resist death. Your thoughts are not My thoughts. The only way for you to even hear My voice is to lay down your "self," your rights, your desires, your ways, and your thoughts. When you are empty, then I can speak. When you are empty, then I can be your LIFE. Knowledge and training are good, but I am looking for the life who lives according to the Truth. I am the Way, the Truth, and the Life. Am I your life today?

> You see, you were created to abide in Me and to be of one mind with Me.

SCRIPTURE
Further Reference: John 5:39-40

Brokenness

You have been broken. You had a lot of strength before, but inner strength that comes naturally brings only false security. Anyone who seeks Me must be broken of their own strength; then they discover My strength. My strength only comes through a broken vessel.

Paul was a man of great strength — physically, mentally, and emotionally. But he had to be annihilated, and he was. Now my church follows his teachings, but do they comprehend the passion of his broken life? How he had to be taken and "unlearn" all the things he had endeavored so mightily to enforce? Can you imagine his heartbreak over My children he had killed?

This heartbreak was real, and it needs to be real in those who follow Me. To see yourself as you truly are is a gift from Me. I allow you to see your frailty, and your own powerlessness, and your own inability to do anything apart from Me. Human nature will fight this truth, but those who are able to receive it will enter into a position of abiding in Me that provides rest from their own efforts.

I break down to NOTHING that which I desire to build.

You cannot be strong apart from Me. Any warrior knows where his strength comes from, because he knows what is in him. He has come face to face with his deepest self in light of My grace and My glory.

You cannot break yourself. Brokenness only occurs by My hand. I arrange circumstances in the lives of My children so they die to their own will. How is this accomplished without pain? How is it managed without heartbreak? If I could do so, how I would! How I would lavish My gifts without reservation, but how shaky human nature is! And how strong is the Tempter! The one who overcomes is the one who does not love his or her life to the death. Power over the enemy comes in death. I conquered in death, and I break down to nothing that which I desire to build.

SCRIPTURE
Further References: Jeremiah 9:23-24; John 12:24-25; Philippians 3:10

Shelter of the Most High

"Jesus, who am I?" *You are My daughter, My child.*
"What do I do today?" *Rest in Me, for I am with you and I am yours.*
"I am sick and in pain, Lord" *That is okay. The answer is the same. Rest in My love for you. Do not allow circumstances to dictate or determine My love for you. Those in the greatest pain are those in position to receive My greatest grace. My heart always sides with the weak and broken of My people. It never sides with the strong and proud.*

Learn this deep within you, My child. A child is absolutely dependent upon Me for everything. To rest in My love you must become like a child. Receive all from My hand, good and bad, and dwell in My love for you. When you arrive at this point of rest, no one or no thing can touch you, especially, your enemy. For you are truly in the middle of My hand. This is what is meant by the shelter of the Most High.

> Those in the greatest pain are those in position to receive My greatest grace.

His Love Comes as a Raging Storm

There is always Love to celebrate, as long as the Love is Mine. I am always at work, always speaking in My gentle whisper, always calling hearts to come and walk with Me by the River of Life. The reason many do not see or sense My presence in the world around them is because they are still looking with human eyes. Many times, I chastened My closest followers for their unseeing eyes and their unbelieving ears.

This is the reason I sent My Counselor. He is ready to teach, to guide, to show you things that are dear to My heart. I long to share My heart, to simply sit down and sup with you. All you must do is open the door to your heart. Every day I am waiting. And every day you must open it and give Me entrance. My deepest treasure is you. My deepest love is you.

I know that your trials have been severe. And I know that you have cried out for My mercy. My heart longs for you when you pull away. I know the temptations of the flesh, and the attacks of My enemy. But it is only through the fire of enduring great temptations that a heart is purified. When the storm is at its fiercest point, you may think that I have abandoned you. But this is only the enemy's deceptiveness, and the frailty of the flesh. If you hang on to Me even though you do not sense My presence, you will come through the storm, and you will become more gentle, more humble, and more still.

I love you, My friend. You must never forget this. My love comes as a raging storm at times, but I will never fail to come in and refresh you, once the storm has passed. As long as you turn to Me, I will always turn to you.

An Iron-Clad Will

There must be in you a strength of will, a strength of determination, and a strength of purpose. This is a strength that far outweighs anything you have ever met in a person before. Many of My people are weak in their wills, and they cling to this weakness as a sign that I will be their strength (2 Corinthians 12:9). But Paul is not writing about a weakness of will. His weakness was the thorn in his flesh I allowed, to drive him to utter dependence upon Me. But in his will, in his purpose, in his determination, Paul was one of My strongest.

I cannot work My fullest purpose in one who has a weak will. Your will must be iron-clad, for you will face much opposition from without. How does your will become strong as iron unless it is forged within circumstances that will melt and consume anything that is less than iron? Your will must be trained to always side with Me. Your will must always be stronger than your emotions.

Your will must seek to be perfectly aligned with My Father's will. And where did My Father's will take Me? Through rejection, scorn, humiliation, torture, and death. I am the Lamb who teaches you meekness, but I am also the Lion who trains your will to be fierce in its intensity.

Why did I say, "Wide is the door through which many will travel?" Because not many make it through the narrow door, for they cannot stand up under the pressure. They don't realize that I allow great opposition to rip away their fleshly nature. Great pressure comes against My saints, not so they will be destroyed, but so they will be purified.

SCRIPTURE
Further References: Matthew 6:10, 26:39; John 6:38, 10:27

Tune Into My Power

Satan is smart. He'll find your weaknesses and come in. Ask Me for wisdom to see how he is operating in your life, and I will show you. I'll never keep you blind. Whenever you think you have him figured out, he'll come in another door. Self-determination will not keep him out. Only reliance on Me — constant hourly and daily reliance on Me — will keep him out. If you feel pride or confidence in any area, he'll move right in.

As long as you are in your body, he will have the power to buffet you. But each of you have the power to defeat him. You just have to be constantly aware of, and constantly in tune with, My power.

Do not allow the enemy to fool you. As you draw near to Me, I will show you things in your life that need to be removed. But you will not lose. I will give the greatest happiness, peace, and joy that you could ever have. One day, you will look back on those things you thought you needed to be happy, and you will see the incredible change I worked in your heart.

> You just have to be constantly aware of, and constantly in tune with, My power.

Some of you will change instantly; others will need to stand at My throne every day and ask for the power to change. Keep asking and I WILL GIVE.

Tune into My power. Don't waste your time on things that don't hook you into My power. Once you get glimpses of real communion with Me, you will not even be tempted to waste any more time.

Union With Me

You have to die to all the ways you learned to live throughout your lifetime. As a child, you needed Me to nurture you, but you didn't know I was there. So you received imperfect human nurture. That is okay.

But never lose sight of My love. In everything that happens, I only want you to die to yourself and open yourself up to My power. I want to use you, dear one. Some people are so driven by their "self" that they never experience the communion with Me that I offer.

I offer you union with Me. This is a deep but very mighty concept for you to grasp. So many of My followers will leave this world still struggling with control over their lives. They will never experience "union" with Me; therefore, neither will they experience My power.

SCRIPTURE

"I am the vine, you are the branches. He who abides in Me, and I in him, bears much fruit; for without Me you can do nothing." (John 15:5)

"And what is the exceeding greatness of His power toward us who believe, according to the working of His mighty power which He worked in Christ when He raised Him from the dead and seated Him at His right hand in the heavenly places." (Ephesians 1:19-20)

Further References: Galatians 2:20; Philippians 3:10

I offer you union with Me. This is a deep but very mighty concept for you to grasp.

Come Away With Me My Beloved

I know you feel that your cross is too heavy for you to carry. But you must know this: you are never closer to Me than when you are on the cross. It is here that I invite you to share in the footsteps of My sufferings. The cross takes you out of your natural life and catapults you into My presence. There is no quicker way. Embrace My cross and I am there.

> True selfless love is willing to lose all for the sake of the Beloved.

My people look for signs and wonders as evidence of My presence. I am looking for the man or woman who lays down his or her very life in order to follow in My footsteps. My broken one knows an intimacy that can never be taken away. Intimacy through pain is the price of love — true love, that is. True selfless love is willing to lose all for the sake of the Beloved. My beloved, follow Me in the darkness and your cross, and I will make your pain one with My pain. Your suffering will establish a depth within you that will be revealed on that day.

Remember, sorrow lasts for a night, and I promise joy in the morning. You may wonder, how long is the night? Well, My precious one, trust me with the unknown length of your night. We have forever, My love. Your morning will come right on time — for My purposes here on earth, as well as in My eternal Kingdom.

Wait For Me

I am leading you to a place that is "above." Sometimes it may seem you are flailing your arms all about, simply trying to stay afloat, but I tell you, "You are learning what it means to depend upon Me. You are learning that, apart from Me, you can do nothing."

You say to Me that you feel as though you are failing. But I say to you, "Even though you are being tumultuously blown about, tossed up and down, you are learning that unless I come through the door on which you are knocking, you will not survive."

This is My job, little one, this is My job: to pull you through. You have done what you needed to do; you have let go of the reins of your life. You have dropped them, and now you are flailing about. But take notice, your eyes are upon Me. I am about to pick you up and carry you downstream. You must realize that it has taken much process to bring you to this point.

I have worked many wonders in your life. You are more than a conqueror. It takes much breaking for you to realize how futile your self-effort is, and that is why you are blowing about in the winds of change. Don't worry. I'm getting ready to pick you up and carry you, My friend. You have proven your devotion to Me and now I am getting ready to show Myself to you.

I will act on behalf of the one who waits for Me. I am your miracle, little one. Wait for Me and do not act on your own behalf. Wait — I am coming.

> It takes much breaking for you to realize how futile your self-effort is.

The Road is Narrow

The road is narrow. The road is narrow. The flesh cannot squeeze through it. I'm calling you up, My child. I'm calling you up.

You must recognize that things — people, places, or circumstances — are not as they appear. The Spirit of Truth underlies the grid of reality that is before your eyes. This is why you must see beyond what you see — you must see with My eyes. You must hear beyond what you hear — you must hear with My ears. Do not be deceived by what appears to be obvious. There are many realities going on at one time in the lives of My children. But you must ask, what is the true reality? What is the one pure reality? What is My heart's view of this situation?

> Do not be deceived by what appears to be obvious.

SCRIPTURE
"Sanctify them by Your truth. Your Word is truth. As You sent Me into the world, I also have sent them into the world. And for their sakes I sanctify Myself, that they also may be sanctified by the truth." (John 17:17-19)

"And we know that the Son of God has come and has given us an understanding, that we may know Him who is true." (1 John 5:20)

Embrace the Cross

You would do well, My friend, to embrace the cross. There are many who are living for Me, but there are few who are dying for Me. The crowd comes running and says, "we want to live," but I say, "Do you want to die?"

Come now, do not keep your brother from death by exhorting him to "have faith and believe." Many are called, but few are chosen. Many can have the faith to believe, but few have the courage to face the pain and loneliness that death brings.

"O death, where is thy sting?" There is no sting to the one who has died. Do not keep your brother or sister from dying with your vain exhortations. Death of self is good, My friend. It is the only way to the life I offer you. Don't you see that it is much better to die than to live? Pray that the eyes of your heart will be enlightened. Help your brother die, instead of hanging on to his life. Help your sister face the cross, instead of giving her the false illusion of life that the flesh brings. Come now, know Me in My death.

Don't you see that it is much better to die than to live?

Are You Ready?

Are you ready to live a life that is founded on freedom? Are you ready to live a life that is founded on rest?

Before you answer "yes" and declare that you are ready, I must present you with another set of questions: Are you ready to live a life that is not driven by yourself? Are you ready to live a life where you have given up all control? Are you ready to live a life that has no name and receives no recognition?

This is the life I am waiting — even longing — to give to each of you. Can you imagine that there are no boundaries to the freedom and love I am ready to give you? You can't imagine this eternal life I hold in store for you, but you can taste and see. Taste and see, and drink Me in until you are overflowing. Measure by measure, one day at a time, you can dive deeper into My sea of freedom.

> Are you ready to live a life that is founded on freedom?

At times, My presence will overwhelm you in such great waves that you will literally be catapulted further into My divine freedom. At other times, you will take steps one at a time toward greater and greater freedom. And out of My freedom flows love, joy, and peace ... free for your taking. Free for your taking.

All across the earth, my body is being awakened into greater freedom. The beauty of My redemption plan is that you will all press in together.

SCRIPTURE
"That they may be made perfect in one, and that the world may know that You have sent Me and have loved them even as You have loved Me." (John 17:23)

Faith

Ask them: When My healing comes, will they want to walk in Me or walk in themselves? I release faith to you according to your ability and your desire to receive it. If you say you want what I have for you, you must be willing to let go of the "known" and embrace the "unknown."

I am getting ready to release "new identities" for My people. I am preparing you right now to receive them, but much fear of the "unknown" still holds My people back. Faith is the opposite of fear, and I will release faith to you according to the measure of your seeking.

Holy Fear

You do not realize it right now, but you are in the midst of several storms. Your faith is pleasing to Me, but it had to be tried and proven in the fire. And, though you are not yet out of the fire, you are standing more securely in the midst of it.

I am forging you like iron, and there will come a time when you can actually see with spiritual eyes the storms raging around you, and you will be vessels of My strength and refuge.

Remember, that which you fear, you seek to please. So, you must seek a fear of Me that reduces all other fears to nothing. No affirmation from any man could come anywhere near My affirmation of you. Holy fear will spur you on to such consecration in your lives that you will gain deeper and deeper knowledge of My affirmation.

And, not only will you know it, it will dwell upon you.

Greater Love

"Greater love has no one than this, than to lay down his life for his friends. You are my friends if you do whatever I command." (John 15:13-14).

This is the "greater love" I am calling you to. This is the "greater love" by which you will be recognized as My people. Whoever desires this "greater love" can receive it; you must simply be willing to lay down your life.

> You are not your own. You can live either in acceptance or in defiance of this truth.

If you are obedient to do so, then you will know My cross. Do not run away from My cross; run to it, for although My cross is a place of pain, it is also a place of safety.

The cross is your refuge, for on the cross, your fleshly nature dies. All your ambition, all your self-seeking, even all your "good" desires will die on the cross. On the cross is born "the best," but you must receive it as My best, not for what it appears to be on the outside.

My cross is rarely lovely, nor is it considered admirable to most. But on the cross, you begin to see with My eyes and feel with My heart. You enter into the understanding that, if you choose to walk "the way" of the cross in this world, then I can be your life. You will walk with a joy deep within you, for joy comes when you are set free from your self. Truly your self is your greatest enemy to walking in communion with Me.

Walking in the way of the cross will bring you wholeness — not just wholeness that comes from emotional healing, but wholeness that comes from spiritual freedom.

You are not your own. You can live either in acceptance or in defiance of this truth. The choice is yours — every day — but once you begin to obey, I will establish a lifestyle within you that emits the fragrance of the "greater love."

Childlike Simplicity

Come now, let me teach you more about my love. My love does not deny reality and the messiness of situations, but it does call forth truth within them. My love propels the beauty inside to the surface. This is nothing short of a miracle as you are steeped within a carnal nature and tossed about by circumstances of continuous warfare.

To grow up you must first grow down.

But this truly is the life hidden in Me. To walk in great responsibility with a light heart is a gift from Me. It does not come overnight, and it is only maintained with childlike simplicity — carved deep within your being. To grow up you must first grow down. To take on more, you must take on less. Do you understand this concept? Are you willing to have me work it into your life?

SCRIPTURE
"Now thanks be to God who always leads us in triumph in Christ, and through us diffuses the fragrance of His knowledge in every place. For we are to God the fragrance of Christ among those who are being saved and among those who are perishing." (2 Corinthians 2:14-15)

Further References: John 3:30; Colossians 3:3-4

Absolute Beauty

I am learning, Lord. I am learning what it means to want You over everything else in my life, to want you over recognition and affirmation (these are truly the big ones).

What is it, Lord, that You have in store for us? Can we imagine? I know we cannot even come near to imagining it, but can we taste it? Can we taste it here, Lord?

Yes, My child, you can taste it. That is truly why I created you — to drink and eat of My very body. My body is living water and nourishing bread. Those who hunger will receive, but receiving Me while you are in your earthly body means receiving My judgment as well as My love. I always correct in love, but many who say they want Me are not yet able to receive Me. They are afraid of My correction because they do not yet know Me as Perfect Love.

I am Absolute Beauty, Total Perfection. If you desire to drink of My very body, you will receive correction as easily as you receive love. They will flow out of Me according to your need at the moment. You may think you need correction and I may pour out only My love. You may think you only need love. However, I may find it necessary to send correction along with My love. My desire is that you know Me as the Perfect Lover. I only correct you because I see in you the beauty you are called to be.

> I only correct you because I see in you the beauty you are called to be.

To see what I see in you is to glimpse the hope of your calling, and it will cause you to run to Me in all-out abandonment. A mere glimpse will enable you to passionately respond to My correction, for you will know that I only desire to bring out the true beauty in you.

Having a sober view of yourself will remove the temptation of spiritual pride, as well as false humility.

Know who you are, My child. Know who I am. Such truth does not come easily, for you must hunger and thirst after My righteousness. But I will not withhold Myself from those who hunger for a full revelation of who I am.

SCRIPTURE

"He who has My commandments and keeps them, it is he who loves Me. And he who loves Me will be loved by My Father, and I will love him and manifest Myself to him." (John 14:21)

"Do not cease to give thanks for you, making mention of you in my prayers: that the God of our Lord Jesus Christ, the Father of glory, may give to you the spirit of wisdom and revelation in the knowledge of Him, the eyes of your understanding being enlightened; that you may know what is the hope of His calling, what are the riches of the glory of His inheritance in the saints, and what is the exceeding greatness of His power toward us who believe, according to the working of His mighty power which He worked in Christ when He raised Him from the dead and seated Him at His right hand in the heavenly places." (Ephesians 1:16-20)

Eternal Violence

Remember, the degree to which you will walk in Me is determined by the degree to which you embrace My cross.

When you choose to embrace My cross daily, you are choosing to say "No" to your self-nature. Your self-nature always stands in opposition to Me, and that is why the very essence of the cross is to bring you freedom to walk in Me.

If you say "Yes" to Me daily, you will enter into the new life that I hold out to you. But you must remember that years of training have produced within you a self-nature that is deeply ingrained. I want to "undo" those years of training and "undo" them quickly. But to do so will take a radical willingness to say "Yes" to Me — because, to say "Yes" means that you welcome my crucifying process. There is a crucifixion I want to accomplish within you that your soul nature would never say "Yes" to. Only your spirit man can say "Yes," and doing so will require an eternal violence from within. An eternal violence reaches with all of its might for that which is pure, holy, and true.

> An eternal violence reaches with all of its might for that which is pure, holy, and true.

I am looking for those who will reach with all of their might. I am looking for those who choose to live for eternity, who will radically say "No" to the ways of the world and the nature of the self. I am looking for those who will say, "I must have all that God has for me, and I am willing to wait. I am anxiously yearning and boldly straining towards the goal for which He has called me heavenward."

No Flesh Can Survive

"But seek first the kingdom of God and His righteousness and all these things shall be added unto you." Matthew 6:33

The very circumstances that are crushing you outwardly and putting pressure on your inner man are intended to mold you even deeper into Me.

In order to even survive the pressure that is upon you, you must have your roots so deep into Me that nothing distorts your vision or shakes your purpose.

Your purpose is given by Me, and your part is to walk it out with all of your heart, mind, soul, and strength. You have no option to be lukewarm or passive; if you are, you will die. You must be red hot or you will not survive, for the very nature of the circumstances upon you will crush anything that is not burning hot with My purpose.

That is not failure on your part; it is the glory of My part, for my glory cannot fall upon your flesh. I am jealous for all of you, and it is My jealousy that has brought you here.

> You must have your roots so deep into Me that nothing distorts your vision or shakes your purpose.

SCRIPTURE
Further References: Hebrews 12:27-29; Exodus 34:14; Leviticus 20:7, 26; Revelation 3:16

I'm Calling You

Don't you see that you do not need to understand what is going on right now? You have done too much trying to understand, to "figure things out" in your life. I am calling you out of that whole way of being; I am calling you into the world of the spirit. You have to let go of all the ways you used to handle life. By "figuring it out in your head," you still have control, right? Or perhaps you just allow yourself to get busier, trying to calm any sense of uneasiness or lack of control by running every which way, adding to your schedule, working harder, trying to fill the void of uncertainty with anything you can think of.

> You need to function in Me and in My spirit.

And when you are through, you still have that deep, abiding sense of uneasiness — a longing. It's a longing for Me, and what you need to do, My children, is come to Me. Your old ways of handling things will not work. You are headed into an arena where you will fall flat on your face if you are not solidly "in Me." You need to function in Me and in My spirit. You will never survive if you try to walk in your power, in your ways of doing things. Just rest in Me, seek Me, yearn for Me. I am here.

SCRIPTURE
Further Reference: Matthew 11:28-30

Closer in the Pain

You find yourself in the midst of deep and burdensome pain right now. The questions I ask you are these, are you growing closer to Me? Am I becoming more and more of your "All in All?" Am I the One you arise in the morning to speak to? Am I the One whose thoughts you are focused upon when you lay your head down at night? Am I the One you partake of daily, even if it is in silence and solitude? Am I the One you seek in the midst of your pain or do you seek to escape from the chaos of your present circumstances?

It is Me, My beloved. It is Me that you must see beyond the veil of your pain, beyond the veil of your circumstances. It is Me that you must see through everything that enters your life.

If your gaze is pure, you will see Me. You will see My love for you. You will see My desire to be one with you yes, even in your pain. Especially in your pain! For in your pain, your flesh is rendered dead. It has no control, no understanding, no rights of its own.

So if you answer "yes" to My first question "are you growing closer to Me in your pain," then the pain is serving its purpose. Welcome the pain, My friend. Welcome it like a cherished friend, for it can do nothing other than drive you deeper into Me. If I could only let it pass, I would. But how else am I to be united with you, My Beloved? How else are you to know the depths of My passion for you?

My Father's heart met you in the cross. Will you meet Me in the cross I offer you? Will you say yes to all of the breakings I must bring to you in order to make you Mine? Fully, completely, 100 % Mine? What Glory!

Be Strengthened in Your Heart

Many times I will take My followers through the things that they fear the most. You must go through pain in order not to fear it. What is it that you fear the most? Do not be surprised if I take you right into that which you fear.

As you go through the very circumstances which you have a fear of, you are forced to make a choice. You either retreat in fear or you advance in courage. There may be moments when My presence appears to not be with you, and these are moments of great formation.

"Even though I walk through the valley of the shadow of death, I fear no evil, for you are with me." (Psalm 23:4) I must ask you My dear friend, "What is it that you fear? Do you fear no evil?"

There is much dread to come upon the face of the earth. Those who are faint of heart will grow cold. Now is the time for you to be strengthened in your heart. Be strengthened by Me. When I allow your circumstances to be such that you are tempted to great fear, that is when My grace will be made available to you. Grace to have courage, grace to trust Me in the midst of all the darkness.

Those who desire to be part of My unstoppable force must go through much tribulation. You will encounter much opposition in your path. Opposition whose intent is to stop you.

You must realize that right now you are in a fight over your very destiny. Do not give into the temptation to fight in the flesh, but learn how to fight in the spirit. You must be forceful. Your resolve to advance must become like iron. Your resolve to believe in what you do not yet see must become solid. In the face of all odds, are you going to believe? In spite of all evidence to the contrary, are you going to believe?

Anyone can believe in what they can see or sense on the horizon. Anyone can believe in that way. But you are being asked to believe in what has slipped further and further away from your sight in the midst of the warfare you are undergoing. Don't be dismayed though — the greatest warriors are those who look to Me against all evidence that I have deserted them.

My child, you must believe as much in the darkest of times as you believe in the lightest of times. I am teaching you this, showing you this, and I will make it possible. Rise to meet Me, Oh discouraged heart, and I will never fail you! I am longing to come to you, but My delay is for sovereign purposes, unknown to you — only to be revealed in the time to come.

> What is it that you fear the most?
>
> Do not be surprised if I take you right into that which you fear.

A people of faith. A people of no fear, trained by the crucible of affliction and tossed about mercilessly at times, only so that what remains will be pure.

SCRIPTURE
"And from the days of John the Baptist until now the kingdom of heaven suffers violence, and the violent take it by force." (Matthew 11:12)

Further References: Deuteronomy 31:6-8; Joshua 1:9; Daniel 12:3; 2 Timothy 1:7-14, 2:1

Reduced to Nothing

You, who have abandoned yourself to all of My dealings. Do not try to take a shortcut out of the pain, but go through it and let it bring you to Me for truly I am your All in All you just never knew it. Until now you might have proclaimed it, but did you live it deep down in your heart?

It is My mercy My child, My Mercy that has brought you here. For truly, would it have been loving of Me to allow you to live a life far below where you were created to live? Would it have been faithful of Me to allow you to live half-hearted when the depths of whole heartedness were available for your taking? Oh My beloved, whole-heartedness can only come to the heart that's been broken of all its ways and healed of all its dividedness. This is the heart I am longing to form in you, My friend. To recreate your heart according to its original intention, a divine masterpiece. A heart made in the image of My Father. A heart created to feel all He feels, including the fathomless depths of His love.

> Wholeheartedness can only come to the heart that's been broken of all its ways and healed of all its dividedness.

This is why you find yourself in such pain right now, My friend, so that through your pain your heart may be made whole unto Me. So it may be undivided in its affections, its focus, its purpose.

Suffering

Too many of my people do not know what it means to suffer for me. It is my suffering ones that are issued this special invitation: To come and sit alongside of me and allow me to crush their hearts into tiny pieces. For only the heart that's been crushed can steward the Love of my Father's heart. Only the heart that has been crushed. Only the heart who knows what it feels like to be forsaken.

Those who fellowship with Me in My sufferings will fellowship in My Joy.

Those who fellowship with Me in My sufferings will fellowship in My Joy. Those who submit to have their heart crushed into fine powder, these are the ones who will receive my Father's Heart in place of their own. Oh, my Beloved Ones, how I long to give out the riches of our Love!

SCRIPTURES

"That I may know Him and the power of His resurrection and the fellowship of His sufferings, being conformed to His death." (Phil 3:10 NAS)

"If anyone loves Me, he will keep My word; and My Father will love him, and we will come to him and make our abode with Him." (John 14:23 NAS)

"But to the degree that you share the sufferings of Christ, keep on rejoicing, so that also at the revelation of His Glory you may rejoice with exaltation." (I Peter 4:13 NAS)

Enter Into My Rest

There is a rest that I am bringing my people into. A rest that takes great effort to arrive at, but the effort is only necessary because of your human nature. Great effort is required to pursue Me at all costs. Pursuing me means purposefully denying everything else. The way of passivity undoubtedly leads to bondage, yet there is a parallel bondage of activity, marked by the yoke of self-effort. Is your effort of a fleshly nature or a spiritual nature? One will lead you into deeper bondage while the other will lead you into my rest.

As I am bringing you into my rest, you will be released from your mind's activity and promoted into the realm of the spirit. This is the realm where you can lift your wings and soar with my wind behind you. And though you will move in great exploits for my kingdom, you will dwell in a state of rest. If you earnestly desire this level of promotion, I will give it to you, but it is only given to those who pay the price at every stage they find themselves walking through. "Such a high price," you may say. But I say to you, "It is not a high price for those who can see where they are going." Ask me for a glimpse of where I desire to take you and of what I desire to give to you. I will enlighten the eyes of your heart to see the hope and the destiny that I have for you.

> Pursuing Me means purposefully denying everything else.

What you seek is simply to know me and to be known by me; to love me and to be loved by me. This isn't something you need to accomplish or strive after. It is a sweetness that settles deep down in your soul. You are who I created you to be. You are nothing less than all that I see and all that I call forth as time unravels. Let my sweetness flow over you now. You are free. Free to be who I created you to be. Nothing more — for that is self effort. Nothing less — for that is passivity and bondage. Come and walk this path of freedom. Come and enter into my rest.

Life Lost is Life Found

The reason many of My people do not find their life in Me is because they are unwilling to lose their life for My sake. To lose one's life; to literally lose everything that has brought one identity, peace, joy, purpose, is far more painful than most can handle. Because it is so threatening to one's basic existence, many will choose to hold onto what they know as life.

> To lose one's life … is far more painful than most can handle.

If only they would trust My words, to lose all, they would find their life in Me. If only they could face the nothingness and pain for just a brief period, they would find all they wanted or needed in Me. And in Me they would receive their new identity. This is what is meant by Matthew 16:25, *"For whoever wishes to save his life will lose it; but whoever loses his life for My sake will find it."*

SCRIPTURE
Further References: Galatians 2:20, 6:14

My Wind is Blowing

There is a strong, steady wind coming … a wind that will blow firm against your back.

Until now, you have been trained by the winds of adversity. Until now, you have known much resistance. But you have learned to stand firm; you have learned to focus on the unseen.

Such learning was necessary, for it prepared you to receive the wind that is coming. Only those who live by the Spirit can sense the wind and receive its power. The flesh cannot discern it, and the flesh cannot run with it. It is too powerful; the flesh will be run over by it. But those who are trained by My Spirit will live by my Spirit.

Look for Me … Look for Me … listen for My voice like the changing of the wind. I am the first and the Last, the Unchanging One, but I am always bringing you into change. You must change if you want to move with Me.

I will change you from glory to glory, if you will only begin to yearn for Me as I yearn for you.

SCRIPTURE
Further References: John 3:8; 2 Corinthians 3:18

AUTHOR'S NOTE

As I underwent the final editing process of the devotional section of this book, I was taken aback by two revelations. One was difficult, but the other was exciting. As I compiled writings from the early years, I noticed a marked difference in style, content and personal expression coming forth. I noticed a judgmental spirit as well as a tendancy toward self-effort. My writing style was more constrained and not as free.

As I poured my heart before the Lord regarding this matter, He made it clear to me that I had been on a journey (as the title notes) and my journey was apparent even in my writings. My heart became softer and more broken through the process, and the Lord helped me recognize the beauty of seeing "where I was" to "where I am" now. Yet I know that He has only just begun!

While I was convinced immediately to discard a few of the early writings, I haved decided to leave the majority of them. Therefore, if you noticed a marked difference at times, you will enter into a more personal experience of this warrior-poet's journey. Enlarging a narrow judgmental heart is nothing short of a miracle, and for this reason I say "Hallelujah to the Lamb of God!"

Truly, His wilderness is a masterpiece in design!

DEVOTIONAL
WRITINGS

Follow

"Seek the Lord and His strength; seek His face evermore!" (Psalm 105:4).

Lord, I know You are not abandoning me when I can't sense Your presence or hear Your voice. You have only stepped further ahead, Your hands beckoning me to follow. "Come further, My child," You say.

But, because I am undergoing such a severe trial, I think at first that you are cruel to remove Your presence. Now, though, I see just the opposite: You love me so much, You desire to build up my character and strength.

> I delight in pure hearts, and I have promised that 'they shall see God.'

You force me to dwell in the darkness, with no one and nothing to turn to for direction or consolation — no one but You. And because I can't sense You or feel You, I must dwell in pure faith, and I learn that what I once called "faith" now becomes "true faith."

You force me, with all that is within me, to look to You and Your strength. You force me to seek Your face with the fervency of a mother bird seeking food for her young. She will die trying to find morsels to put into their weak, helpless little bodies. She has only one mission, and she will not rest — not even slacken her pace — until she completes it. This is what she lives for. She has no purpose other than her mission, no identity apart from it.

Are you stumbling around in difficult circumstances? Are you afflicted in ways that drain your energy and make you want to give up? Take heart. These trials do not "cancel you out," for Jesus has entrusted you with purpose. The darkness is part of His path for you. Simply accept it as such, and allow Him to lead you.

"I see your desire to live for Me. Now I will take you further. You can trust Me. When you can't see Me, just follow My voice; when you can't hear Me, just follow My heart. As you do this, you will learn to walk by faith and not by sight. The more you walk by faith, the less you depend upon yourself … and the less you depend upon yourself, the more you depend upon Me.

"I cannot use those ruled by self. I delight in selfless love, and I will do whatever I will to bring My true followers out of themselves and into Me. I delight in pure hearts, and I have promised that 'they shall see God.' Purification of the heart takes time, and sometimes it comes about quite painfully. You must realize that the things I take from you are not eternal. They may appear to be crucial at the time, but eternity is so far from t his earthly realm. You can only carry into eternal life what you have cultivated in the Spirit.

"Do not miss My opportunity. Do you desire to share in My holiness? Do you desire only My best? Then do not resist. Trust Me, and let Me lead."

SCRIPTURE
Further References: Jeremiah 32:39; Ezekiel 11:19; John 6:63; 1 Corinthians 3:10-15; Hebrews 12:9-14; 1 John 3:2-3

Hope

Psalm 147:11 says, "The Lord delights in those who fear Him, who put their hope in His unfailing love." My hope is not in doctors and medicine, nor in vitamins and nutrition. It is not in others, my church, or myself. My hope cannot be in my own discipline or in my determination to make things better.

I need to follow where He leads, and not follow man, or knowledge, or even wisdom. I must follow the Way, the Truth, and the Life, Jesus Christ Himself. If He leads me down a dark path, I will follow. If all looks bleak to my physical eye, I will follow His voice that speaks to the eyes of my heart. I will neither despair nor fear, for He promises to go before me, fight for me, and — when it seems fit — even carry me.

Sometimes we need to be carried; other times, we need to walk in the darkness, moving only by faith, listening intently to the Shepherd's voice. He determines what we need every moment, and we can rest assured He is working out His finest purposes.

> How our weakness allows His divine power to be manifested!

We may feel we need to be carried, and we may cry desperately for Him to do so. But He sees our heart, and desires to strengthen it (2 Chronicles 16:9). We are not (seemingly) left without help because we are weak, but because our hearts are fully committed to Him. His eyes roam throughout the earth, and when He finds those who are "wholehearted," He strengthens them, sometimes by carrying them, but most often through trials and suffering. Though our outer being is falling apart, inwardly we are being renewed. We may not "feel" His strength when we "need to," but through our weakness, He is enlarging our spirit in unseen and unfelt ways. How our weakness allows His divine power to be manifested!

SCRIPTURE
Further References: Deuteronomy 1:29-31; 1 Kings 8:61; 2 Chronicles 16:9; Isaiah 40:11, 41:10, 43:1-2; 2 Corinthians 4:16-18

The Greatest Gift

"If you sinful people know how to give good gifts to your children, how much more will your heavenly Father give good gifts to those who ask him." (Matthew 7:11 NLT)

What can I ask for my dear Lord, except for union with You? How can I ask for any good gifts – when You truly are all I will ever need?

If I can have You indwell me I will be complete. I will be whole. Ready to go where You tell me to. Ready to speak Your words, to love with *Your* love and *Your* heart. Having no emotions apart from Yours. Is this possible? Is it possible to have only Your thoughts — none of my own — but to be so consecrated that I fully walk in Your will? Is this where Paul walked?

Oh, Jesus do not remove Your hand from me until You do this in me! Oh, Lord, give me the strength until this is accomplished!

Trust

"This is what the Lord says: 'Cursed is the one who trusts in man, who depends on flesh for his strength and whose heart turns away from the Lord. He will be like a bush in the wastelands; he will not see prosperity when it comes. He will dwell in the parched places of the desert, in a salt land where no one lives. But blessed is the man who trusts in the Lord, whose confidence is in Him. He will be like a tree planted by the water that sends out its roots by the stream. It does not fear when the heat comes; its leaves are always green. It has no worries in a year of drought and never fails to bear fruit." (Jeremiah 17:5-8).

Blessed are you who trust in the Lord. Cursed are you who trust in man, who depend upon yourself for strength. Beware of this warning; attend to this promise.

In times of turmoil, what comes naturally to you?

Are you bothered or worried by what lies ahead? Does the threat of tribulation or the end of your present comfort shake your peace? What does your armor look like? Who have you been relying upon for protection? His faithful promises are your armor and protection (Psalm 91:4). It is easy to claim His promises during good times, but times of testing will prove whether we really have staked our entire being and existence upon His faithfulness.

The life of Judah's King Asa (2 Chronicles 16) depicts a man who once received blessings, but in the end was cursed. When Asa relied on the Lord, He delivered mighty armies with great numbers of chariots and horsemen into his hand. But when Asa made a treaty with the king of Aram to gain victory over Israel's king, Basha, God removed His power. "You have done a foolish thing, and from now on you will be at war." (See 2 Chronicles 16:1-9.) I wonder what got into Asa's head. Was he intimidated by King Basha's aggression? Did he just want to maintain his position, and did what came naturally?

In times of turmoil, what comes naturally to you? Will you consistently rely upon the Lord? True, crises are invitations to release God's awesome power, but God will only act for those who trust in His name alone, and rely only on Him.

SCRIPTURE
"Woe to those who go down to Egypt for help, who rely on horses, who trust in the multitude of their chariots and in the great strength of their horsemen, but do not look to the Holy One of Israel, or seek help from the Lord." (Isaiah 31:1)

"Be careful, or your hearts will be weighed down with dissipation, drunkenness, and the anxieties of life, and that day will close on you unexpectedly like a trap." (Luke 21:34)

Further References: Isaiah 12:2; Isaiah 50:10-11

We Live By Grace

"Not to us, O Lord, not to us. But to Your name be the glory, because of Your love and faithfulness." (Psalm 115:1, NIV).

Let us remember: anything He calls and enables us to do is by His power and for His glory.

But self-righteousness is easy to come by. We work hard to please and obey the Lord in every way. Then we look around and we see other believers not working so hard. Perhaps they seem to be giving in too easily to their passions. Or they make mistakes and we assume a little more self-worthiness.

> When we focus our eyes and energy on our efforts, we lose sight of His mercy and grace.

Why can't we more easily recognize the voice of self-righteousness? God never tells us to take credit for anything. Everything comes from God, is carried out through the Holy Spirit whom He supplies, and goes right back to Him. "For from Him and through Him and to Him are all things. To Him be the glory forever!" (Romans 11:36, NIV).

Do we need to be reminded that our righteousness comes through faith in Jesus Christ? When we accepted his salvation, we accepted His justification … and both were gifts of grace. "There is no difference, for all have sinned, and fall short of the glory of God." (Romans 3:22-23). If this was our salvation cry, why do we think we can live apart from the grace of Jesus Christ?

It seems that, as years are added to our initial salvation, we tend to grab some glory for ourselves.

Satan begins to tempt us with smug self-satisfaction, and before we know it, we focus on our best efforts to please God. "It does not, therefore, depend on man's desire or effort, but on God's mercy. For the Scriptures say to Pharaoh: 'I raised you up for this very purpose, that I might display My power in you and that My name might be proclaimed in all the earth.'" (Romans 9:16-17, NIV).

When we focus our eyes and energy on our efforts, we lose sight of His mercy and grace. But all of us stand only by grace. Apart from grace, we will fall; if we live by grace, we will freely extend grace. If we live by our own righteousness, we will judge others by their visible righteousness. "For they being ignorant of God's righteousness, and seeking to establish their own righteousness, have not submitted to the righteousness of God." (Romans 10:3).

Marriages — wake up! Parents and children — wake up! Friends — wake up! Churches — wake up! We can claim nothing as ours, except the grace and mercy and love of our Lord Jesus Christ. Let us walk in it and freely extend it to one another. Then, truly, God will receive the glory.

SCRIPTURE
Further References: John 3:30; 2 Corinthians 4:7-12; Galatians 5:24-25; Philippians 3:9; Colossians 2:6.

Hope to Carry On

"Since, then, you have been raised with Christ, set your hearts on things above, where Christ is seated at the right hand of God. Set your minds on heavenly things, not on earthly things. For you died, and your life is now hidden with Christ in God." (Colossians 3:1-3, NIV).

Sometimes God calls us to recreate our lives according to the eternal perspective He offers us. As we continually reach for "things above," let us reach with all our strength, not with feeble attempts. God is so good, so all-powerful, all-loving, and all-knowing. No circumstance should imprison us, although admittedly, many things in this world will cause us tremendous pain. Prisons can be physical (chronic illness, physical suffering); financial; or emotional (divorce, infidelity, an unbelieving spouse, loss of a job).

But we can never be spiritually imprisoned unless we allow Satan to place us there. God's power that lives in us through His Holy Spirit is endless. His power will uphold us, despite our circumstances —and in the midst of them. "For I am persuaded that neither death nor life, neither angels nor principalities nor powers, nor things present nor things to come, nor height nor depth, nor any other created thing, shall be able to separate us from the love of God which is in Christ Jesus our Lord." (Romans 8:38).

Just when we feel we cannot handle ONE MORE thing going wrong ... when we're at our end and feel we can't make it through another day ... when depression lingers around the corner and we feel it would be easier to fall into a hole, "barely existing" ... then His power gives us the strength, force, and hope to go on. Do you know that Jesus came to give you life more abundantly ... now, even as you doubt that His promise is meant for you here on earth?

God loves us deeply, and His love is at its height when we are at our depths. "Therefore most gladly I will rather boast in my infirmities, that the power of Christ may rest upon me. Therefore I take pleasure in infirmities, in reproaches, in needs, in persecutions, in distresses, for Christ's sake, for when I am weak, then I am strong." (2 Corinthians 12:9-10). We cannot change the walls of our prisons, but we can "soar in our spirit" within those walls, because the natural world cannot contain the supernatural. Jesus is alive in you, and as you dig deep into His living water, He will give you a peace that transcends all human understanding. (See Philippians 4:7.)

> God loves us deeply, and His love is at its height when we are at our depths.

Ah, the unseen miracles that take place every day! Sure, healings and changes in physical circumstances happen in response to prayer and faith in God's power, but the greater healing occurs in the one who allows his or her inner spirit to be stretched, strengthened, and enlarged so that the natural man has less and less control in his or her life. (See Romans 8:29.)

Be ever thankful, therefore, for the things that cause your outer man or woman to relinquish control, to surrender your reign over your life, to allow the Spirit of Jesus Christ to reign more and more fully. You may have asked Jesus into your life when you were broken and in need. Is there brokenness in your life right now? Hallelujah! Praise Him! He seeks to claim more and more of you.

SCRIPTURE
Further References: Romans 8:28-39; James 4:7,10; 1 John 5:14-15

Pay Attention

"My son, give attention to my words; incline your ear to my sayings. Do not let them depart from your eyes; keep them in the midst of your heart; for they are life to those who find them, and health to all their flesh." (Proverbs 4:20-22). "To fear the Lord is to hate evil; I hate pride and arrogance, evil behavior and perverse speech." (Proverbs 8:13, NIV).

I want the Lord to look at me and be pleased. I don't want Him to see anything He would "hate." I want to have listened to His words. When I am at the end of my life, I want Him to look at me and say, "You heard Me. You listened to My voice amidst the world's clutter, your own good desires, your need for approval and acceptance." I want Him to say, "You heeded My words and did not lay up treasures for yourself here on earth."

I want my heart to be in the right place. I want to live Matthew 16:24-28 in whatever way God desires. I want to be led with the eyes of my heart, a heart of faith, and with ears opened to the Master's voice. I want to live in daily communion with Him, sensitive to His leading, while desensitized to my own.

"Then Jesus said to His disciples, 'If anyone desires to come after Me, let him deny himself, and take up his cross, and follow Me. For whoever desires to save his life will lose it, but whoever loses his life for My sake will find it. For what profit is it to a man if he gains the whole world, and loses his own soul? Or what will a man give in exchange for his soul? For the Son of Man will come in the glory of His Father with His angels, and then He will reward each according to his works.'" (Matthew 16:24-28).

SCRIPTURE
Further References: Proverbs 4:20-27, 6:16-19; Matthew 6:19-21

The Warrior is a Lover

It is right for you to take time just to be with Him; after all, He created you for Himself, and He created you for love.

Your heart is truly that of a warrior, for you see the work that needs to be done. He is pleased with you, for you have not shrunk back. You are determined to answer His call to set the captives free. You have stood firm in the attacks sent against you. You have grown in wisdom, discernment, and knowledge of the enemy's tactics.

But know that His most courageous warrior is also created for love. There are times when you must lay down your weapons and simply sit at His feet and allow His love to wash over you, pour into every wounded fiber of your being, and heal you.

You are His beloved. "I am my lover's and my lover is mine." (See Song of Solomon 6:3). Do you know what it means to be "His" — uniquely and specifically "His"? Know that the ultimate warrior is also the consummate lover. He is compelled to war because of love, and he is driven to love because of the war.

He longs for you to simply adore Him … to kiss His feet … to come to Him for no reason other than to come to Him. "For love is as strong as death, its jealousy unyielding as the grave." (Song of Solomon 8:6, NIV). He is jealous for you. In heaven, we will be found worshipping Him without end. Come, worship Him right now!

> Know that the ultimate warrior is also the consummate lover.

Identity in Him

Many of God's children think that they are suffering for His will, when they are simply suffering from a lack of discipline. Some days we will feel the emotional high of fellowship and love in Jesus' presence. Other days, we feel only our flesh, or perhaps just don't "feel" His presence. Any devoted follower, however, must be disciplined in will, thought, and emotions. The problem begins when we doubt His presence because we do not sense it. When we begin to wonder, we begin to suffer, because a wondering mind is a "wandering" mind. Our faults are so large that we feel incredibly inadequate to change or eradicate them. This is when we need to simply "come to Jesus."

We must never forget that we live in a fallen world in a mortal body with a fallen nature. When all we can see and all we can feel are our human thoughts and emotions, then we need to acknowledge our absolute powerlessness, and simply "come" and "abide."

> You can only walk in this freedom when you walk in the truth about yourself.

During these precious moments, Jesus is calling us to our IDENTITY in Him, although we tend to think the opposite. When we are flowing in service and love to others, we take on this "output" as our identity. But these times of overflow and service are actually the result of an intense longing for His presence. Like a stranger in a foreign country, we earnestly look forward to the city for which we are destined. Jesus can only fill up His vessels when they know their desperation and neediness apart from His power. We must know and understand our "jar of clay" Jesus hand-picked for our residence. No two of us are alike, yet all of us are called to be like Jesus. Identity in Him is established only when "self" has no identity.

"He who loves his life will lose it, and he who hates his life in this world will keep it for eternal life." (John 12:25). Why do you think Jesus uses a word as strong as "hate"? This verse remains a mystery to many of His followers throughout their lives. But Jesus told us that we would "know the truth" and the truth would "set us free." When you know the truth, accept it, abide in it, and then you will be free. You can only walk in this freedom when you walk in the truth about yourself.

SCRIPTURE
Further references: John 8:32; Philippians 3:8:14, 4:19; 2 Corinthians 4:7; Hebrews 11:9-10; 1 Peter 1:13

God's Judgments are Sent to Purify

There is a suffering that comes from disobedience and a suffering that arises out of obedience. While the former can be viewed as chastisement or discipline, the latter is better described as purification or refinement.

> Difficulties we experience as believers could be divinely-sent judgments intended to purify us.

We must be certain to know the difference. God gives us discernment so we can understand our own particular trials and sufferings. But He has not given us permission to judge what type of suffering others are going through. We need to rest assured that God alone searches all hearts and examines all of our inner motives. He will give each person what he or she deserves.

The first step to discerning our suffering is to submit to God and then resist the devil. As we humble ourselves before Almighty God, He will reveal where our hands need to be washed of sin and our hearts need to be purified of hypocrisy. Discipline can become purification, but only if we sincerely seek what God is trying to teach us by allowing us to suffer.

We must encourage our suffering brothers and sisters, but we must be careful not to intercept God's plan in their lives. Often, we are too quick to be compassionate and comforting, and we immediately pray 'the difficulty' away. But the Lord's purpose is to draw us to Himself and make us holy. "But as He who called you is holy, you also be holy in all your conduct." (1 Peter 1:15).

Difficulties we experience as believers could be divinely-sent judgments intended to purify us. We need not fear them, and we certainly must not resist them. If we try to rise above them in our own strength, God will resist us even more. But if we humble ourselves as God desires, He will give us the grace necessary to endure.

There is only one thing for us to do: commit ourselves to our faithful Creator and suffer according to His will and His timing. Embedded deep within our hearts must be the knowledge that He will lift us up in due time as we humble ourselves under His mighty hand.

SCRIPTURES
Further References: Isaiah 1:19-20, 25-26; 48:17; Jeremiah 7:10, 13, 23-28; James 4:7-8; 1 Peter 4:17, 19; 5:5-6

Dealing With Pride

Ecclesiastes 3:1-8. There is a time for everything, a season for every activity under the sun. Yet Scripture does not tell us "there is a time to be humble, a time to be proud," because there is never a time to be proud. At all times, in all ways, we must be humble—about ourselves and about our circumstances.

There is nothing healthy or "acceptable" about pride, if we are to become consecrated followers of our Lord. Many accept Jesus as Savior with a fully developed stronghold of pride. After all, to function within the world and survive effectively on our own, we learn to hear the voice of self and self-preservation.

> To deal with pride in any way other than crucifixion is to compromise the commitment Jesus asks of us.

There is only one solution: THE CROSS. To deal with pride in any way other than crucifixion is to compromise the commitment Jesus asks of us. "You can enter God's Kingdom only through the narrow gate. The Highway to Hell is broad and its gate is wide for the many who choose the easy way. But the gateway to life is small, and the road is narrow, and only a few ever find it." (Matthew 7:13-14, NLT).

Are you seeking to take the narrow way? Or is your self-pride too much of an obstacle for you? Examine your life right now, and consider whether you are holding out in any area, relationship, or attitude that is not humbled under the mighty hand of God.

The most dangerous strongholds are not the obvious ones, and unfortunately they are the ones we too easily excuse among ourselves as fellow believers. "Righteous anger" is one label we throw around loosely when Scripture says our righteous acts are as filthy rags. (Isaiah 64:6). We feel justified denouncing our spouse, and harboring bitterness, when he or she has genuinely wronged us. Yet Scripture says love is patient and doesn't keep account of wrongs suffered (1 Corinthians 13: 4, 5). We talk about growing in our faith and going to the next level, but Jesus says, "Whoever desires to become great among you, let him be your servant." (Matthew 20:26).

"Unless you change and become like a little child, you will not enter the Kingdom of heaven." (Matthew 18:3, NIV). Have you humbled yourself lately? If so, how quickly did you fall into pride again?

In John 13, Jesus, preparing to wash the disciples' feet, chooses to begin with Peter. "No, you shall never wash my feet," exclaimed Peter. He carried a mixture of humility (he did not want Jesus to perform this lowly service for him) and pride (he tried to dictate Jesus' behavior). Even his next response, although wholehearted, still dictates to Jesus. "Then, Lord, not just my feet but my hands and my head as well!" But Jesus had no desire to clean the whole body, and once again Peter misses the point. Do we sometimes miss the point like Peter? Are we a mixture of pure devotion and self-centeredness?

JOURNAL ENTRY:
There is a great demand on the chosen ones of God. He requires everything, and nothing less.

Acquiring Faith

"So do not throw away your confidence; it will be richly rewarded. You need to persevere so that when you have done the will of God, you will receive what He has promised. But My righteous one will live by faith. And if he shrinks back, I will not be pleased with him." (Hebrews 10:35-36, 38, NIV).

Salvation cannot be earned, but faith must be acquired. My friends, I encourage you not to shrink back when trials and suffering come, and not to take the easy way out.

Our Maker loves us beyond comprehension. If only we realized that we can please Him. We can bring to Him our every problem, trial, persecution, and suffering. As our Great High Priest, He understands our weaknesses and sympathizes with our pain. Each time we come to Him, He is there to meet our need. But once we have poured out our heart to Him, He leaves us with a choice. We can choose to trust in the reality we see and feel, or we can trust in Jesus, the firm and secure Anchor of our soul.

He offers the hope, but we must do our part in reaching out and taking hold of it. Brothers and sisters, be greatly encouraged that, in times of trial, we can take another step up the ladder of faith. He always waits with His offer of hope. The question is, will we reach out and grab hold of it?

SCRIPTURE
"This hope we have as an anchor of the soul, both sure and steadfast, and which enters the Presence behind the veil, where the forerunner has entered for us, even Jesus, having become High Priest forever according to the order of Melchizedek." (Hebrews 6:19-20)

Further References: Isaiah 25:9; 50:10.

Glory to Glory or Death to Death?

The Christian life is not hard to live — if we walk in humility and fear the Lord. It is hard only if we walk in pride and fear our fellow man.

Those living the first kind of life spend no energy trying to "establish one's self;" the latter work constantly at it. A life of humility walks with no walls, is quick to confess and repent, and allows God's Holy Spirit to freshly flow in. A life of pride uses much energy to maintain walls of self-preservation, and is never secure without the acknowledgment of others.

Where is your energy going: to self-preservation or self-annihilation?

The former's life progresses from glory to glory, because it is so sensitive to the Spirit's prompting that it does not hesitate when it hears the Voice whisper, "This too must die; here again you must lay down the way you think it should go." The latter's life goes from death to death, because, ironically, it refuses to die. It actually says "No" to the very door that would open it to life.

Where is your energy going: to self-preservation or self-annihilation? In your life, is trust more evident than fear? If we all know that the first way of living fuels us with the Lord's resurrection power, why do we hold on so tightly to our lives and our pride?

Is uncertainty so scary? I would rather live by Jesus' power with nothing certain in my life than to live a life that deposits a death stench wherever it goes. (Ephesians 5:2). All too often, we mistake another's death stench as the Spirit of God if it brings comfort to our own death stench. This may be why our lives exhibit so little of God's glory.

Maturity Through Perseverance

"Because you know that the testing of your faith develops perseverance. Perseverance must finish its work so that you may be mature and complete, not lacking anything." (James 1:3-4, NIV).

Mature, complete, lacking nothing. Do you want to be mature? Then ask the Lord to work His perseverance into you. But, when you ask, be sure you can accept what He brings your way, and allow Him to finish His work, without taking back your request. Perseverance is willing to wait and willing to endure. It undergoes any pain, hardship, or loss in faith and in hope. No matter what means God may take, the end result is worth the cost. Maturity: "attaining to the whole measure of the fullness of Christ." (See Ephesians 4:13.)

> Perseverance is willing to wait and willing to endure.

The cost will entail the testing of your faith, and probably a refining of your hope. Who are we if our faith has not been tested through trial? These trials have come "that the genuineness of your faith, being much more precious than gold that perishes, though it is tested by fire, may be found to praise, honor, and glory at the revelation of Jesus Christ." (1 Peter 1:7). Who are we if we have not been called upon to prove our faith? A faith that is tested will prove to be genuine. In Genesis 22, Abraham is tested to the utmost when he is asked to sacrifice his one and only son. Yet his faith is made complete by what he did. He did not withhold his one and only Son.

How will you respond when your faith is tested? Will you shrink back in fear, or will you accept the opportunity to prove that what you profess is real?

Next, will your hope prove to be real? Many of us use the word "hope" loosely. It is one thing to hope for something we can see or sense already on the horizon. It is another thing to hope in the face of all odds, in the midst of all-encompassing darkness, in the case of one disappointment after another, after another, after another.

The refinement of our hope usually entails some kind of discipline. We rely too much on what we can see and touch, but God will take us beyond what we can see to make us "fix our eyes on Jesus, the Author and Perfecter of our faith." And yet, God's hope cannot be "worked up" by man's effort. It is His gift to us by His Holy Spirit. (Romans 8:24-25; 15:13). We are usually brought to the end of ourselves, and we must wait in longing for that which we desperately desire. It is then that God infuses us with His hope, coming in like a fresh breeze after the storm.

Finally, perseverance is not possible without the hope that God's promise in Romans 8:28 will be fulfilled. So, dear ones, you who seek maturity and desire to be strong in character, know that God will take you on a path where you will crumble if your faith and your hope are not genuine. Some of you right now might be on this path. Some of you may not have invited God to work His perseverance into you, yet you find yourself in such a trial. Well, then, as James says, consider it pure joy, my brothers and sisters, for God has seen to it to make you mature, trained to distinguish good from evil (Hebrews 5:14), lacking nothing, and ready for anything that lies ahead.

SCRIPTURE
"For when the way is rough, your patience has a chance to grow. So let it grow, and don't try to squirm out of your problems. For when your patience is finally in full bloom, then you will be ready for anything, strong in character, full and complete." (James 1:3-4, Living Bible)

God Glories in Empty Vessels

One day when I was having a difficult time with my physical circumstances, I implored the Lord for insight. "Lord, you said that if we believed, we would see the glory of God (John 11:40). Well, I believe, Lord, and I've been believing You now for a long time, waiting to see Your glory. Why haven't I?" After a period of silence, the Lord led me to reflect on humility. If humility is taking no thought of one's self in light of one's accomplishments, then one should also take no thought of one's self in light of one's failures — or, as in my case, one's sufferings.

> God is looking for hearts that will trust Him with all-out abandon.

The abandoned, humble soul is ready to accept, without resistance or question, whatever comes from God's hand. The Lord is looking for a soul that is neither easily excitable nor easily deflated by circumstances. He is looking for a soul that thinks nothing of itself to such an extent that it receives misery as easily as it receives the Master's bountiful daily bread. He is looking for a soul that doesn't flinch at all when the Master leads it down a darkened path — because it has learned to plant its feet upon the Rock of Confidence. Confidence that isn't necessarily bold and outgoing but carries a meekness about it that can say, along with Job, "though He slay me, yet will I trust in Him."

God is looking for hearts that will trust Him with all-out abandon, even when He gives no reassurance whatsoever. He is looking for hearts that acknowledge that all human insight and knowledge are nothing in the light of His infinite wisdom and majesty.

When I came to this revelation — that He is everything and apart from Him I am nothing — I heard His response to my question, "My child, you are looking for the glory in the form of a miracle, but I AM THE GLORY. I never withhold Myself from the vessel who is empty."

Oh, precious Lord, help us understand the depth of Your love for us, and how deeply Your heart seeks to fill us. Teach us these truths: that You are looking for empty vessels to pour into; that you created us for You, and You long to give Yourself to us; but that You will never force Yourself upon human nature. How can we prepare for You, when all of our thoughts, ways, ideas, and concepts fall far short of Your glory? How can we prepare for You except by emptying, dying, becoming nothing, so that You can be our all? Oh, Lord and Savior, have mercy upon us, and be our glory. In Your precious and holy name we pray.

SCRIPTURE
"And said, 'Truly I say to you, unless you are converted and become like children, you will not enter the kingdom of heaven. Whoever then humbles himself as this child, he is the greatest in the kingdom of heaven.'" (Matthew 18:3-4)

Refiner's Fire

"'And it shall come to pass in all the land,' says the Lord, "that two-thirds in it shall be cut off and die, but one-third shall be left in it: I will bring the one-third through the fire, will refine them as silver is refined, and test them as gold is tested. They will call on My name, and I will answer them. I will say, "This is My people;" and each one will say," The Lord is my God."'" (Zechariah 13:8-9).

You will not find many lukewarm Christians in the middle of the refiner's fire. The Lord makes Himself available to all His children, but He meets us according to our desire to meet Him. Do we desire to have all that we can of Jesus Christ and His indwelling power? The Lord seeks those whose hearts are truly surrendered to His Divine Will and Purpose. When He finds someone with that kind of heart, He delights in meeting his or her obedience with His purifying fire. "While every branch that does bear fruit He prunes so that it will be even more fruitful." (John 15:2, NIV). Our God is a consuming fire, and He will permit nothing within us that is inconsistent with His nature. "Without holiness no one will see the Lord. See to it that no one misses the grace of God ... see to it that you do not refuse Him who speaks ... for our God is a consuming fire." (See Hebrews 12:14-15, 25, 29).

> Our God is a consuming fire, and He will permit nothing within us that is inconsistent with His nature.

For those of us who say we truly love Him He will show Himself to be a jealous God, pruning here, testing there, afflicting one area, and speaking judgment to another.

Believers who seek Him with all their heart will find Him. But on the journey, they will undoubtedly encounter His purifying fire and His rod of judgment.

Believers, let us seek Him now, so we may be judged in the body and purified while there is still time to radically live for Him. Let us call disobedience what it is and not act as if we are suffering for the will of God. Parents discipline their children, so the children will not be snared in their disobedience. Do you want to be hindered from His best?

"But who can endure the day of His coming? Who can stand when He appears? For He is like a refiner's fire and like launderer's soap. He will sit as a refiner and a purifier of silver; He will purify the sons of Levi and refine them as gold and silver, that they may offer to the Lord an offering in righteousness." (Malachi 3:2-3). Those who desire the Lord's coming must know that clean hands and a pure heart are required. This is how He desires to meet His Bride. Are you seeking the obedience that leads to purification? Are you enduring gracefully the fire He has in you — like clay in the potter's hand?

Taking Hold of Eternal Life

"God is light and in Him is no darkness at all." (1 John 1:5). All of our thoughts, our emotions, our actions ... do we lay them before the spotlight of Jesus' love? Every regenerated believer contains pockets of rebellion hidden underneath layers of obedience and submission. Whenever the Spirit nudges us on what needs to change, we quickly rattle off all the ways we have been obedient, or how far we have come from where we used to be. Fellow believer, let us realize that God will only work with us as far as we are willing to go. "For the eyes of the Lord run to and fro throughout the whole earth, to show Himself strong on behalf of those who heart is loyal — fully committed — to Him." (2 Chronicles 16:9).

> Fellow believer, let us realize that God will only work with us as far as we are willing to go.

As Paul declares, we have not already been made perfect, and we should never consider ourselves to have yet taken hold of that for which Christ Jesus took hold of us. "Straining forward to what is ahead, I press on toward the goal to win the prize for which God has called me heavenward in Christ Jesus." (Philippians 3:14, NIV). Beloved, let us join Paul. Let us STRAIN forward to what lies ahead. Let us PRESS ON to take hold of the eternal life to which we are called. Right here, right now, we can claim its benefits in greater fullness. As Paul said to Timothy, we can take hold of life that is "truly life."

May you seek to make your goal the same as Christ's goal for your life. Let us discard all He reveals in us that is not in union with His

Majesty. "He who is not with Me is against Me." (Matthew 12:30). Let us commit today to be with Jesus in all that we are — our innermost thoughts and our deepest motives. If you hear His gentle voice today, I urge you not to harden your hearts. Be quick to run in response to His words and throw off anything that hinders Him from having ALL of you.

SCRIPTURE
Further References: Philippians 3:12-14; 1 Timothy 6:12, 19; Hebrews 6:1; 1 John 1:5

The Great Breaking

There is a great breaking coming among God's people. Many of His people have endured circumstances that were intended to break them. But they have pushed through the circumstances clinging more deeply to their self. So they have come through unchanged with their self stronger in the process.

The time is growing shorter. We cannot let one more day go by without fully living in surrender to the One who abides within. "Be very careful,

> Be very careful, then how you live … making the most of every opportunity …

then how you live — not as unwise but as wise, making the most of every opportunity, because the days are evil. Therefore, do not be foolish, but understand what the Lord's will is." Ephesians 5:15-17. Every day, have in the front of your mind what the Lord's purposes are. Have foremost in your heart the desire to fulfill the Lord's will on earth as it is in heaven, and the consequent decision to lay aside your own will.

Have You Considered the Costs?

"So likewise, whoever of you does not forsake all that he has cannot be My disciple." (Luke 14:33).

Paul declares that we have been set free from sin and have become slaves to righteousness. Paul spoke of nothing less than a wholehearted way of living. You are either a slave to impurity or a slave to God. He doesn't say that sometimes he is a slave to righteousness and sometimes a slave to God. Are we guilty of lowering the standard when it is convenient for us? Do we let Jesus have ALL of us sometimes and a LITTLE of us at other times?

> Jesus chose us to bear His fruit, and once He has met our need, He calls us to meet His needs.

Many of us surrendered to Jesus because we realized only He could meet our needs. We were desperately in need of a Savior. But, my friends, that is only the first step of eternal life. Jesus has needs that can only be met by us.

Jesus chose us to bear His fruit, and once He has met our need, He calls us to meet His needs. "You did not choose Me, but I chose you and appointed you that you should go and bear fruit, and that your fruit should remain." (John 15:16).

We are the vessels through which His Holy Spirit has an outlet into this world of darkness. Are you available, through wholehearted surrender, to be a servant of God — going where He tells you, speaking His words of Truth, loving with His *agape* love, renouncing all rights to yourself? If so, you will be His light in the world. You, indeed, will be His friend, because you have considered the costs and are obeying His commands. "You are My friends if you do whatever I command you." (John 15:14). Brothers and sisters, Jesus became a servant for us while we were yet sinners, and then He gently, yet firmly, invites us to be His friends. "No longer do I call you servants, for a servant does not know what his master is doing; but I have called you friends, for all things that I heard from My Father I have made known to you." (John 15:15).

Will you accept the INVITATION? You accepted Him for what He could do for you; are you ready to say "yes" to what you can do for Him?

SCRIPTURE
Further References: Luke 14:28-33; John 14:12, 15:12, 14; Romans 6:15-23

He Offers Us Freedom

He stands with His hands outstretched, offering freedom to you and me. This freedom is without price to us, for money cannot touch its wealth. Yet it will cost us all. To receive this freedom, we must give Him everything. A believer will never be fully free with ambition tucked within a corner of his heart, or with pride hidden under the surface, ready to jump out if threatened. We must come cleansed of all self. To some this is nearly impossible, and they will never taste His freedom. He will give them glimpses, He will whisper quietly to woo them, but they will not come to Him for absolute freedom, because the price is too high. They will choose to remain shackled to the world, to their flesh, or to the enemy of their soul.

What pain this brings to the Savior's heart! I urge you to take notice within you. As Paul beseeches us in Romans 12, in view of God's mercy, offering our bodies as living sacrifices — heart, mind, and will — is our first act of worship. Let us not be content to give our money, but hold on to our selfish ways. Let us not be satisfied with serving according to our comfort, without surrendering our whole self to His infinite design.

We must know that freedom is waiting! We must know that He offers the "richest of fare." Today, let us turn to Him and let the veil fall away. He can remove whatever is keeping you from feasting with Him now.

SCRIPTURE
"Come all you who are thirsty, come to the waters; and you who have no money, come, buy and eat! Come, buy wine and milk without money and without cost. Why spend money on what does not satisfy? Listen, listen to Me, and eat what is good, your soul will delight in the richest of fare." (Isaiah 55:1-2)

Further References: Psalm 36:7-9; John 4:13-14

Realness

Lord, everything You allow is to glorify You, but if we do not acknowledge it to You — lift it back to You — how can You take the messes of our lives and mold them into Your handiwork? Who am I fooling by trying to cover it up, be positive, "put on the makeup"? You want us to offer ourselves as "living sacrifices" on Your altar. Well, all of "ourselves" means all of our emotions, all of our sorrows, all of our frustrations, all of our questions, all of our inadequacies. THEN You can use us. THEN You can restore us, strengthen us, heal us, change us.

O God, perhaps my biggest failing has been to think performance matters to You. Only realness does.

God's Grace

Any sense of pride or self-accomplishment needs to be burned out of us in order for God's Spirit to have its full reign.

As we draw nearer to this point, we are also growing more and more in awareness of our own sinfulness, pride, and weaknesses. How can God have more of us if we don't first surrender what needs to go?

Don't feel bad then when you see your sinfulness flash itself rudely into the picture of your life. Don't be dismayed with the thought that you have such a long way to go in meeting Jesus' command to be perfect. (Matthew 5:48). Instead, thank God that His grace, that draws you by the hand and leads you alongside the greatest of all sinners, refuses to allow you to be deceived. Then, in freedom and truth, you can exclaim with Paul, "O wretched man that I am! Who will deliver me from this body of death? I thank God — through Jesus Christ our Lord!" (Romans 7:24-25).

Do You Fear the Lord Above All Else?

"He will be the sure foundation for your times, a rich store of salvation and wisdom and knowledge. The fear of the Lord is the key to your treasure." (Isaiah 33:6, NIV).

If fearing You, O Lord is the key to our treasure, why do we hear so little about it in our churches? On the contrary, it is easier to recognize the fear of man ruling in the hearts and lives of believers. In some believers, the fear of man completely directs their decisions and actions. In others, it may creep up every so often. However, God's Word doesn't talk about an "in-between." Either we fear the Lord or we do not. The fear of God cannot drive our lives only on Sunday, nor can it be compartmentalized. It must undergird our home, work, marriage, child raising, tithing, and serving. There can be no doublemindedness in the one who fears the Lord. Either He will be the cornerstone of our lives or He will be our greatest stumbling block. (Isaiah 8:11-15).

> How deep is your need for approval? How afraid are you of rejection?

"And now, O Israel, what does the Lord your God ask of you but to fear the Lord your God, to walk in all His ways, to love Him, to serve the Lord your God with all your heart and with all your soul." (Deuteronomy 10:12-13, NIV). Notice how the Lord first of all asks us to fear Him. Fear Him ... and then walk. Fear Him in order to love Him. Fear Him in order to serve Him. Fear Him in order to observe His commands.

That which we fear, we will seek to please. If we cannot handle disapproval, then we will seek to please a disapproving man or woman, a family, corporation, or "body of believers." How deep is your need for approval? How afraid are you of rejection? If you are concerned about disapproval from any source other than the Lord, then that is what you will fear.

Or perhaps you fear hurting someone else's feelings more than receiving disapproval. You shrink back from speaking the Truth in love, but by doing so, you are telling God His Truth has limits.

Are you willing to be disliked? Hated? Disowned? "All men will hate you because of Me, but he who stands firm to the end will be saved." (Matthew 10:22, NIV). We will meet with disapproval, not only in the world, but even in the body of believers. Brothers and sisters, we must fear God above everything else. To fear Him is to receive His wisdom and knowledge. It is to place the desire to please Him at the VERY CENTER of our beings. (John 8:29). It is to make Him our foundation, our choicest gold, our only source, our only Hope, our only ALL in ALL.

SCRIPTURES
"Oh, My child, that your heart may be inclined to fear Me ..." Deuteronomy 5:29, NIV)

Further References: Psalm 2:11, 19:9-11, 86:11, 103:11; Proverbs 1:7; Isaiah 50:10-11, 51:12-16; John 5:30; 1 Thessalonians 2:4.

Climbing the Mountain

There is a rough and ragged way that affords little rest — to the body, mind, and soul. It is a way that demands absolute commitment simply to ensure survival. It is a way that affords no luxury and even seems to dispute the very mercy of God. At every turn, one finds harassment from the enemy, conflicts from the world, fears and insecurities from within. No feeble heart will make this journey, for above all else, it is a test of one's heart.

If you hunger deeply for the Lord, He may take you on this way. As powerfully as you desire Him, His desire for you is unfathomable. He cannot contain His love for you and His desire to draw you near. Therefore, He chooses the quickest path for you to come closer to Him, to know Him intimately. He takes only those who are willing on this tumultuous path; He will lead His other children up the mountain in a more gradual way. You may see a little incline, followed by a rather long plateau, followed by another incline, then a plateau, and then, perhaps, a minor decline. The decline is simply a result of the comfort the plateau brings. The long way is long because comfortability tends to make one lukewarm and passive.

> No feeble heart will make this journey, for above all else, it is a test of one's heart.

The measure of a man or woman is often revealed by the road he or she chooses. We wish we could get to Him an easy way, but His purposes are very clear. It is the process of the climb that rips against our flesh and kills it. Only the Spirit can provide the strength and continual impetus to keep climbing in the midst of tribulation. Who can endure this steep and narrow way? Only the humble, for only they can see how much further they have to go. Pride looks down and sees how far it has already come.

The traveler on this ragged road will see more ugliness within himself than will the one on the road of comfort. He may be tempted to yield to great despair or at least much discouragement. Take heart, dear one, for the Lord does not see what you see. The Lord sees a diamond in formation.

Tempted To Lose Heart

Is exhaustion a part of the journey we must make in these bodies of flesh? Were the Israelites tired in their journey through the desert, going three days without water? Was David more than likely exhausted at times in his anxious, running escape from the hand of King Saul? Did Paul get exhausted during his missionary journeys, having to endure constant pressure, hardships, distresses, beatings, imprisonment, hunger, and sleepless nights?

> But we must come to Him to be our supply, trusting Him to carry us and uphold us.

The Son of God endured His greatest temptation at His most vulnerable point. It was after 40 days and 40 nights of wearisome fasting that the tempter met Him in the desert. Scripture tells us, "He was hungry." (Matthew 4:2). It was there that God who became man, who possessed the means to end this temptation, chose to endure the test. In doing so, He cut a path far above our human possibilities, surpassing all our human impossibilities and offering us His divine power.

When we think He's asking too much from us, and we just cannot take another step or stand firm in our faith, then His power can come in. But we must come to Him to be our supply, trusting Him to carry us and uphold us.

Where are you now, dear believer? Do you feel God is asking too much? Is your earthen vessel breaking under the load? Paul had many breakings in his earthly life, yet he wrote: "Therefore we do not lose heart. Though outwardly we are wasting away, yet inwardly we are being renewed day by day." (2 Corinthians 4:16, NIV). "Wasting away outwardly," yet they do not lose heart. Are you wasting away? Are you tempted to lose heart? Then know that this is where the resurrection life of Christ can come in. Can it come in any other way? Search the Scriptures for yourself. Read and meditate on the lives of David and Paul. Heroes are not born in luxury or even in mild distress; they are forged in the fires of great tribulation and severe emotional and physical suffering.

SCRIPTURE
Further References: 2 Corinthians 4:7-12; Philippians 3:10-11

Undivided Hearts

"Then I will give them one heart, and I will put a new spirit within them, and take the stony heart out of their flesh, and give them a heart of flesh ... and they shall be My people, and I will be their God." (Ezekiel 11:19, 20).

We all are wounded people needing healing from the enemy's lies and strongholds. We need healing to be free, but once free, we face a dilemma: Who are we going to be?

> An undivided heart is not acquired overnight, nor is it acquired by picking and choosing one's deaths

When God called His people out of Egypt, it took Him 40 years to transform them from slaves into sons and daughters. Obedience is hard to learn, and we in the church are not exempt from our culture's refusal to submit. "Hearts of stone" carry within them roots of selfishness, ambition, pride, love of comfort and pleasure, apathy, and unbelief. Hearts of stone need to be removed, and God is in the process of doing so.

Beware of speaking loosely about this process, because it is anything but easy to our human nature. Dying is painful and God is sounding His call. Who is willing to say "yes" to Him and "yes" to the deaths that the self must undergo?

An undivided heart is not acquired overnight, nor is it acquired by picking and choosing one's deaths. Those who say "yes" and open their arms wide must expect and embrace the deaths that Jesus will bring to them. They also must expect moments of consecration where everything they are and have is rendered completely powerless apart from the power of God.

The more quickly we die, the better. God is rapidly transforming "separate individuals" into "His people." Words like "burnout" and "sacrifice" will not even be in these people's vocabulary. A dead man or woman cannot "burn out," for they live only by the supernatural power of God, which will always supply the one who abides in Jesus. We talk about "sacrifice," but who can consider "sacrifice" the honor of being selected to give our best to the One who loves us the most? What greater privilege could there be? "Greater love has no one than this, than to lay down one's life for his friends. You are My friends if you do whatever I command you." (John 15:13-14).

Hearts of stone cannot access this greater love. Only hearts transformed through many crosses can understand a love that is beyond our natural ability. God wants to pour out His power of Love. Do you want to be one of His chosen receptacles?

Only Through Suffering

Trials are the context for blessings that we receive only by suffering through them. We tend to look at all the losses and heartbreak from our trials. However, in the spirit realm, God is bestowing gifts that not only are unseen at the moment, but gifts which, by their very definition, only come through suffering. "And not only that, but we also glory in tribulations, knowing that tribulation produces perseverance." (Romans 5:3). "My brethren, count it all joy when you fall into various trials, knowing that the testing of your faith produces patience. But let patience have its perfect work, that you may be perfect and complete, lacking nothing." (James 1:2-4). Endurance, patience, and perseverance require the deepest kind of self-denial.

> We cannot stand still in a crisis, because a crisis is a crossroads where we either step up or move backwards.

There is a suffering that is a consequence of sin, but the suffering I speak about has nothing to do with sin or selfishness. "Though He was a Son, yet He learned obedience by the things which He suffered. And having been perfected, He became the author of eternal salvation to all who obey Him." (Hebrews 5:8-9). Not that God's Son was ever disobedient, but He was called on to obey to an extent He had never before experienced. The temptations He faced were very real indeed, and the battle for victory was exactly that — a battle. Denying His own will to the point of death, Jesus won, and His humanity was completed ... "made perfect."

People ask for the gifts of the Holy Spirit. They ask to be placed in a position to be used by God. But how many ask to have the Lord's purposes carved within them? Or shall I say, the Lord's image worked within them? During a trial, the temptation to sin is great. But the battle is won by trusting instead of doubting or allowing discouragement to set in. The battle is won by moving beyond "Why have You forsaken me?" and asking the Lord to mold you like clay and make you more perfect.

We cannot stand still in a crisis, because a crisis is a crossroads where we either step up or move backwards. Painful as it may be, we will never be the same again. We will see with eyes that have a richer view of life as a whole. We will see a little deeper into the human soul, with eyes that are wiser about the real love that was in the Father's heart when He watched His Son die.

SCRIPTURE
"For our light affliction, which is but for a moment, is working for us a far more exceeding and eternal weight of glory, while we do not look at the things which are seen, but at the things which are not seen. For the things which are seen are temporary, but the things which are not seen are eternal." (2 Corinthians 4:17-18)

Are You Living the Spiritual Life?

I am concerned that many of our Lord's followers are not really living at all. I say this because His path to life first goes through death. (John 12:24). In the heart and soul of every believer, God speaks daily about how he or she is to die. (1 Corinthians 15:31). The question is, do we listen to Him? If we listen and obey, then we receive His power for living and carrying out His divine purposes for our day.

Many followers, however, have become desensitized to His voice. One reason is self-sufficiency. If it is primarily our need that draws us to Him, and we are not experiencing any great need in our life, when why would we press in on Him? Isn't it easy to remain content where we are spiritually?

Supernatural power only comes when we are willing to die to control, comfort, our time, our way of thinking.

The second reason is based upon the first. We are too comfortable in having our needs met. We give out of our excess — excess money, time, and energy. We feel good when we give according to our reserve, and by living this way we essentially hold on to our lives. The problem is that when we give out of our excess, our living is meager and we operate on natural power. Supernatural power only comes when we are willing to die to control, comfort, our time, our way of thinking. The one who gives out of excess misses the Gospel message. Any acts of love done in the natural are pitiable, because Jesus said we are not to save or find our life. We are called to hate our life, lose our life, and deny our self in order to take up our cross and follow Jesus. Our self-life must be crucified. When we enter into this kind of living, our power is supernatural and our love is great.

We are called to serve Jesus from the inside out, requiring a total commitment of our entire being. We are not told to take care of all our needs first and then serve Jesus. We are told to seek His Kingdom and His righteousness and He will take care of all our needs. (Matthew 6:33). Why do people with the least seem to have the most to give? Because they have never had the option of selfish living and meager giving. From the start, their circumstances have led them to press in on Jesus with all that they have and all that they are. Their need has made them rich in Jesus; their lack of excess has made them rich towards God. (Luke 12:21).

SCRIPTURE
Further References: Psalm 37:4; Matthew 6:33, 16:24-25, 19:29; Mark 8:34-35: Luke 9:23-24; John 12:24-25

JOURNAL ENTRY:
It is a dreadful thing to fall into the hands of the living God for the person who has not judged him/herself or sought to be purified in the flesh. But for the person who has judged him/herself while in the flesh, it's an awesome thing to fall into the arms of the living God! In fact, there is no better place!

What is Your Joy?

What a blessing to be united with Christ! Do you know that suffering is one of the tools God most uses to help us learn joy? We tend to think it is the opposite. We "feel" joyful when things are going well for us, when we experience certain blessings in our journey of faith. We "feel" joyful when we are on a mountaintop, not in the valley.

But when I look in God's Word, I find wisdom directing me in an opposite direction. Blessed are those who are poor, who are hungry, who weep, who are hated, excluded, insulted, and rejected. "Rejoice in that day and leap for joy! For indeed your reward is great in heaven." (Luke 6:23). Paul says, "I am exceedingly joyful in all our tribulation." (2 Corinthians 7:4). And again in 2 Corinthians 6:3-10, Paul commends the servants of God who endure trouble, hardships, and distresses of all kinds. "Sorrowful, yet always rejoicing."

> Do you know that suffering is one of the tools God most uses to help us learn joy?

"Dear friends, do not be surprised at the painful trial you are suffering ... but rejoice that you participate in the sufferings of Christ, so that you may be overjoyed when His glory is revealed." (1 Peter 4:12, NIV). "Participate" means "to enter in, alongside of, join in." Trials are our opportunities to do experientially what we do by faith when we accept Christ. By faith we unite ourselves with Christ, accepting His death as our death to sin and to self. United with Him in death, we are united with Him in resurrection. Praise God for inviting you to participate in sufferings, because in suffering you have a multitude of opportunities to die. In suffering you have an invitation to unleash Jesus' resurrection power within you.

We are called to die daily, but how many of us obey that call? Beloved children, suffering is a tool God uses to assist us in embracing His cross. Only by embracing His cross do we truly live, and this is why we rejoice! God wants us to truly live, to live united with His Son. Not just as an intellectual fact, but as a living reality.

Ask someone where his or her joy comes from, and the answer will tell whether it is the joy Jesus proclaims to His lost world. Ask yourself, "Do I know the joy Jesus talks about?" Not just the joy of being saved *from* sin, but the joy that is set *before* us. "Let us fix our eyes on Jesus, the Author and Perfecter of our faith, WHO FOR THE JOY SET BEFORE HIM, endured the cross, scorning its shame, and sat down at the right hand of the throne of God." (Hebrews 12:2 NIV). Jesus' joy was accomplishing our eternal redemption and receiving honor and glory at the Father's right hand.

What is your joy? Is it to be united with the Father through Jesus Christ, by dying to self, in order to glorify Jesus through your human temple? If this is your joy, then you may be one who finds yourself in a valley according to the visible eye. But I encourage you, ask God to enlighten the eyes of your heart. He wants to show you His mountaintop. And believer, what better place could there be?

Chosen Calling

"His mother, Mary, was pledged to be married to Joseph, but before they came together, she was found to be with child through the Holy Spirit. Because Joseph, her husband, was a righteous man and did not want to expose her to public disgrace, he had in mind to divorce her quietly." (Matthew 1:18-19).

Ponder this for a moment. To the world, Mary's pregnancy looked like a curse; to Divine eyes, it was a chosen calling. To the men and women of that day, Mary's situation would have been a scandal; to the heavenly hosts who had the honor of witnessing the unveiling of the Father's plan, Mary was His handiwork. She had proven herself worthy of His calling.

> Can we trust God when we hear Him speak, even though we see many complications in the physical realm?

You and I look at Mary now and say, "What an honor to carry the Son of God." But we forget that to Mary's world, she was a disgrace. She received personal assurance from the heavenly angel, but those around her did not. In fact, she didn't even attempt to defend herself to Joseph. He was ready to quietly divorce her, until an angel also visited him in a dream.

I am touched by Mary's simple, unquestioning obedience: "I am the Lord's servant; may it be done to me as you have said." (Luke 1:38, NIV). She didn't say, "What will people think?"

"What will I tell people?" "What will I tell Joseph?" She simply trusted God.

Can we trust God when we hear Him speak, even though we see many complications in the physical realm? Can we trust Him when we hear Him speak, even though we do not like what He seems to be asking of us?

You might say, "If I had an angel visit me, I would obey God just like Mary did." But I say to you: God desires to speak to us through His Word and the power of His Holy Spirit. He is always seeking an opening in the hearts of men and women. I am sure Mary had cultivated the quiet presence of God and learned the art of worshipping Him daily. I am sure she had a tender, submissive spirit. She knew what obedience was. That's why she responded so splendidly when He shocked her with His proclamation.

If you are cultivating His presence, I can guarantee that He is speaking. The question is, what do you do when you hear Him whisper to you in the quiet place? Is your response like Mary's? He will test you with small things before He can give you more. We all look at Mary and think, "What a calling!" Yet the eyes of the Lord roam throughout the earth, searching for hearts who are fully committed to Him (2 Chronicles 16:9), and His desire is to bestow calling after calling upon those who are ready to believe. "Blessed is she who believed that there will be a fulfillment of those things which were told her from the Lord!" (Luke 1:45)

SCRIPTURE
Further References: Matthew 1:18-19; Luke 1:38, 45

What is Faith?

"Now faith is the substance of things hoped for, the evidence of things not seen." (Hebrews 11:1).

Why does God make us wait for that which is so precious to us? Throughout history, mankind has conjured up all kinds of complicated philosophies. However, Jesus' viewpoint is simple: He wants to do uncommon things through common people. How do we, common bodies of flesh, become vessels for the uncommon? By being trained to see with eyes of faith. What is faith if it's easy? Many unbelievers talk about faith in an obvious way: "I have faith that my daughter will grow out of this phase." "I have faith that one of these jobs will come through." But do we as believers think any differently? In Hebrews 11:2, it is written that God gave His approval to people in days of old because of their faith. Would God give His approval of us today?

How do we, common bodies of flesh, become vessels for the uncommon?

Believers, we must be light in the darkness. We cannot walk about speaking "faith" but living "by sight." How much will we further God's Kingdom that way? Maybe a little, but Jesus never speaks in "little" terms. He says the Kingdom of Heaven must be like a mustard seed planted in a field. The smallest of seeds becomes the largest of garden plants. Birds of all kinds will flock to its branches for shelter. (Luke 13:18-19).

How is this faith acquired? God, in His supernatural ways, operates differently in every life. However, one thing is certain:

without a period of waiting, we would not be given the resiliency necessary for a faith that stands against all odds. Without a period of testing we likely would not move beyond a "common sense" faith into a faith that lives, sees, and breathes in accordance with the supernatural power of Jesus Christ. (Ephesians 1:19, 3:30). Our Father desires that we who believe in Him will live our lives according to the "incredible greatness of His power." (Ephesians 1:19, NLT).

Lord Jesus, help us not to walk with eyes of compromise with the world's ways, our vision marred by finite potential. Give us eyes of faith that see into the darkness as beacons of light that draw people to You. Show us what it is to live by Your power, Lord. Increase our faith, Lord. Give us faith that would receive Your approval, O Lord. By Your grace and mercy, we pray.

True Love

There is a true love, and there is a faulty, human love. The true love flows from the river of God as a fresh stream into the depths of our being. How do we obtain this love? By basking in the Author and Creator of Love.

We hear that this Love is patient. How do we, in our earthly nature, acquire this patience? By waiting in the presence of the One who alone knows patience, the One who longs to give us His love. But how can He give if we do not take the time to receive? How can He give if we do not give up our very self and come to sit at His feet? In doing so, we cannot demand "fast food," because we will learn patience as we wait for Him to pour out His richest delights.

He knows the value of true patience. He who does not rush us, but calls us by His love, knows how much we need to be broken of our desire to "have it all" without paying any price. The price to be paid is not for our punishment, it is for our gain in the grace of Jesus Christ. When we are willing to pay the price, we, in essence, are willing to crucify our sinful nature, which knows nothing about patience.

This nature, in fact, knows nothing about true love. It flatters itself with displays of false love, thereby remaining entombed within itself and its own illusions. But the soul that knows true love has a conscience that is uneasy with this wretched means of love. It searches outside itself for that which is deeper, truer, more powerful. The soul on this journey knows that any price — particularly solitude —is nothing compared to receiving the riches of His Love.

Oh, that we would all yearn for this Love that is beyond all our best attempts! This Love is pure, perfect, and all-consuming!

Jesus Removes the Veil

"Come to Me, all you who labor and are heavy laden, and I will give you rest. Take My yoke upon you and learn from Me, for I am gentle and lowly in heart, and you will find rest for your souls. For My yoke is easy and My burden is light." (Matthew 11:28-30).

Sometimes it is easy to come to Jesus; other times, it is nearly impossible. The reason for the difference lies in our self. How big is your "self" today? "In Me your souls will find rest." Jesus will not give you rest until you step out of your self. He always offers His part. Pray that the eyes of your heart will be enlightened, so His Spirit can speak to you. Do you hold bitterness, resentment, pride, anger, or jealousy? If you do, they will act as a veil, blocking His life-giving power.

Jesus cannot remove this veil unless we ask Him to. Once we implore Him to help, totally aware of our own inability to remove something so deeply ingrained in our human soul, He will not hesitate to come and heal us. What human father would hesitate to give a good gift to his child, especially if he held that gift in his hand? (Luke 11:11-13). How much more, then, does our Heavenly Father long to give healing to all those emotions that hold us back from His abundant life.

If we could only glimpse His heart for one second, we would not hesitate to let down our walls and ask Him for His touch or a healing word to set us free.

SCRIPTURE
"Now the Lord is the Spirit, and where the Spirit of the Lord is, there is liberty. But we all, with unveiled face, beholding as in a mirror the glory of the Lord, are being transformed into the same image from glory to glory, just as by the Spirit of the Lord." (2 Corinthians 3:16-18)

Come to Him

Sometimes we need to be renewed (Isaiah 40:28-31; Psalm 119:28). Sometimes we need healing (Malachi 3:2-3; Isaiah 57:14-19). And sometimes we need to press forward (Philippians 3:14; Psalm 119:29-32). Whatever it is, come to Jesus for it and allow Him to do it for you. There is no such thing as passive Christianity. Even when we are resting and waiting on God we are COMING TO HIM, bring our whole self to Him at His disposal. It is an active proclamation to say, "You are all I need; and only You can fill me, only You can heal me." So I say "No" to self-effort, and I say "No" to my self-pride which continually wants to push down my neediness or ignore my gaping wounds. So fearfully clinging to my "sense of control," my inborn pride takes on a life of its own. "Hey, I'm okay. I'm in control. I can handle it."

> There is no such thing as passive Christianity.

Of course God calls us at all times to be strong, but to be strong in Him. And in order for that to happen, we must first bare our wounds to Him. Wounds inflicted by others, wounds inflicted by the world, wounds inflicted by our sinful self. And once the wounds are brought to Him, then He can heal, He can renew. He can build us up in "Him" so that we can truly press forward saying "Lord your grace IS sufficient for me, for in my weakness you are made strong." If we aren't continually being made aware of our own vulnerabilities, our own fallen nature, our incessant need to be "in control," then I do not know how we can profess that He is our strength.

Faith that is Firm

He has called us by name. He has made you and me His very own. He doesn't say that we might pass through some hard times. He says, "When you pass through the waters and through the rivers." Moses had to be willing to walk into the Red Sea, and if God had not parted the waters, Moses would have drowned. But Moses trusted God's character so much, he was willing to die — if that was what God had in mind. When Shadrach, Meshach, and Abednego walked into the fiery furnace, they were willing to be burned. They had to step into the flames in order to be saved. God could have saved them on the outskirts, but that wasn't the Almighty's plan. His plan is that the world will see His glory, and His desire is that the world will see our faith. There is no place for cowards among the faithful remnant. Men and women of great faith must stand firm until the end. "If you do not stand firm in your faith, you will not stand at all." Isaiah 7:9.

"But now, thus says the Lord, who created you, O Jacob, and He who formed you, O Israel: 'Fear not, for I have redeemed you; I have called you by your name; You are mine. When you pass through the waters, I will be with you; and through the rivers, they shall not overflow you. When you walk through the fire, you shall not be burned, nor shall the flame scorch you. For I am the Lord your God, the Holy One of Israel, your Savior.'" (Isaiah 43:1-3).

> There is no place for cowards among the faithful remnant.

SCRIPTURE
Further Reference: Isaiah 60:1-3

Submission or Rebellion?

What path are you on? Is it one of submission, or one of rebellion? Perhaps, if you are honest, it is a little of both. Unfortunately, God never excuses rebellion. His will is neither wide nor easy. "Make every effort to enter through the narrow door." (Luke 13:24, NIV).

Only Jesus lived a life of perfect submission to His Father. Let us examine ourselves. If we find ourselves in the middle of these two heart attitudes, we are essentially carving out our own will in life. True, we are better off than the unsaved soul that goes straight down the road of rebellion, but as believers committed to the life of Jesus, we are falling short of His high calling for our lives.

His will is neither wide nor easy.

Rebellion comes in degrees, of course, and some of us are closer to the submission end of the spectrum. We may be tempted to compare ourselves to those who are closer to the rebellion end, but Jesus never spoke in terms of appeasement. His words are "sharper than any double-edged sword, penetrating even to dividing the soul and spirit ... judging the attitudes of the heart." (Hebrews 4:12, NIV). Jesus tells us that we are to be perfect, just as our Heavenly Father if perfect. (Matthew 5:48). Who can escape the fire of these words? Do we excuse them by stating that, as humans, we can never fully attain such a high ideal? Do we loosely use the phrase "you are too hard on yourself" when we see a fellow believer struggling under the fire of Jesus' words? We all make the choice whether or not we will hold His words up as a barometer from which to judge who we will be today.

SCRIPTURE
Further References: John 4:34, 6:38; Romans 2:5

Inaccessible in the Secret Place

Too many of us are too busy to be of use to God. We run from here to there and our minds are easily distracted by the many concerns we carry. But God has only one concern … to draw us into communion with Him. If we dwell within the Shelter that He offers, we will rest within His Shadow. (Psalm 91:1) To truly say He is our Fortress, we must enter into the REST He provides. His love can only be our stronghold when we draw near to Him. Then He will draw near to us. He will peel off the scales that harden our heart and distract us from what is most important.

Enter into the high walls of His Fort and leave your many distractions behind you. Rest within His Shadow for a while

> Too many of us are too busy to be of use to God.

and leave through a different door. No matter how many or how varied your troubles are, He promises that his faithfulness will be your Shield and your Rampart. When you make the Lord your Refuge, you will become merely a spectator of the war that God will fight for you. "A thousand may fall at your side, and ten thousand at your right hand, but it shall not come near you." (Psalm 91:7). Even though you must go back out into the world, "only with your eyes shall you look, and see the reward of the wicked." (Psalm 91:8). For you will be inaccessible to your enemies in the secret place of the Most High.

SCRIPTURE
"And Jesus answered and said to her, 'Martha, Martha, you are worried and troubled about many things. But one thing is needed, and Mary has chosen that good part, which will not be taken away from her.'" (Luke 10:41-42)

Further References: Psalm 91:1-16; 92:11, 94:16-19, 22-23, 143:11-12.

Your Level of Rest

At what level of rest are you now? Is your rest determined by the circumstances in your life, or by your position? When we abide in Him our circumstances can be turned upside down, and we will not be shaken. Before Jesus left His disciples, He gave them His gift of peace, but He made it clear that his peace was not the same peace as the world gives. "Peace I leave with you. My peace I give you; not as the world gives do I give to you. Let not your heart be troubled, neither let it be afraid." (John 14:27).

> Is your rest determined by the circumstances in your life, or by your position?

The world defines peace as the absence of conflict; this, however, is a "false peace." Christ's coming into this world brought conflict from the beginning, and inevitably brings conflict into the life of every believer. Christ brings peace, but His peace brings conflict — between light and darkness, between flesh and spirit, between sons of the devil and sons of God. As long as the prince of this world remains the prince of this world, he will be bent upon strife and destruction.

Any peace apart from Jesus Christ is a "mirage." Yet we believers often position our rest upon this mirage. Worse yet, our spirit sometimes comes into agreement with this mirage. It is then that we forsake the call of Jesus.

"They are not of the world, just as I am not of the world ... As You sent Me into the world, I also have sent them into the world." (John 17:14, 18). He sends us into the world, but not to be of the world. We are only sent to declare Him. We are only sent to declare the

Truth. As Satan has no hold on Jesus, so he has no hold on us as we abide in Jesus. We have been given His peace, which we are to proclaim to the world.

Before we can proclaim it, however, we must repent of any desire for its counterfeit in our life. Remember, the god of this world is a master of deception, and he tempts us to secretly desire the peace that knows no conflict. And if he succeeds, he disarms us of our greatest weapon: the fire of God. The fire of God cannot stand impurity. Without the fire of God ablaze within us, we all are tempted to anesthetize ourselves against the impurity of the world and the flesh. The fire of God will always draw our spirit into war with the flesh and the world. But we must remember that we do not wage war as the world does. On the contrary, our weapons have divine power to demolish strongholds.

The effectiveness of our weaponry depends upon our position and our precision. "The prince of this world is coming. He has no hold on Me, but the world must learn that I love the Father and that I do exactly what My Father has commanded Me." (John 14:30-31, NIV). Our position of abiding in Jesus will prevent the evil one from having any hold on us. The precision in which we war effectively will be determined by our level of rest — that is, whether we have grasped the peace offered by Jesus Christ, or whether we secretly desire the world's peace. And finally, our level of rest will be determined by how closely we follow in Jesus' steps when He says, "I do exactly what My Father has commanded Me." He calls us to His rest, the inner spiritual rest that is the same in the mightiest battle or in a joyous celebration.

SCRIPTURE
Further References: Matthew 10:34; 2 Corinthians 10:3-6

Entering God's Rest

"For this Good News — that God has prepared a place of rest — has been announced to us just as it was to them. But it did them no good because they didn't believe what God told them." (Hebrews 4:2, NIV).

Do the difficulties of your present circumstances overshadow the reality of God's promise? The enemy's desire is to steal our hope before God fulfills His promise. Have you handpicked one of God's promises for yourself in your present situation? Have you cried out to Him and sought him until He personally replied to you, whether through another believer, His Holy Spirit, or His infallible written Word?

> Do the difficulties of your present circumstances overshadow the reality of God's promise?

When a promise from the Word of God jumps out at you as you seek the Lord, then rejoice and grab hold of it! This is His personal word to you which no one — especially the enemy of your soul — can take away, and most certainly no one can stop from being fulfilled.

There is, though, a period of time between the promise and the fulfillment. This is the danger zone, and some of us must endure great testing as we await the fulfillment of God's word to us. Whether we have to wait a week, a month, or several years, we will be prime targets for the enemy to steal our hope. "Let us do our best to enter our place of rest." (Hebrews 4:11, NIV). Those who enter God's rest will find rest from their own efforts. They will find rest from their impatience, pain, and eagerness. They will find rest from the enemy's badgering.

We must know that the hope is not ours to "muster up." It is not ours to maintain, nor is it in the enemy's power to take away. Hope comes through, and is kept by, the power of the Holy Spirit. The enemy can only steal it if we accept the lie that it is ours to maintain. "Now may the God of hope fill you with all joy and peace in believing, that you may abound in hope by the power of the Holy Spirit." (Romans 15:13).

The only thing we need to do is to fix our eyes firmly on the redemptive power of Jesus Christ. Our best efforts will always fall short. Only the power of God through Jesus Christ can hold us, keep us, maintain us, and shield us as we await what lies in store for us, "who are kept by the power of God through faith for salvation ready to be revealed in the last time." (1 Peter 1:5).

JOURNAL ENTRY:

When I am with Him and I am myself completely, honestly myself — that is freedom. That is when He can speak His whispers of love to me. That is when He can shine upon my face, bestowing upon me grace upon grace. Grace to know His heart for me. Grace to respond to His heart for me. Grace to release all my fear of the unknown and fall deeper into Him.

Building for Eternity

God is always offering you opportunities to step out of yourself. Even doing something as mundane as paying bills, you are offered the chance to dwell in Him or in yourself. You do not have to minister to thousands to be in your purpose; your purpose lies in being conformed to His likeness.

Because you have been born from above, He dwells within you. But He longs to possess all of you — including your mind.

Let Him have your whole mind. He desires to renew it through His truth, and in doing so, He will transform your thought life. The realities and experiences that your mind has collected through the years are filled with lies and misperceptions. He will purify your thoughts by cleansing you of all falsehood.

You must begin to realize that the realities you see with your eyes are on one level. He wants you to see beyond this level, to the eternal reality that undergirds all of life. Your spirit is eternal, and He desires for you to live, not according to the flesh, but according to the Spirit. Your nature is weak, but the Spirit within you is strong, because it is united to Him. Do not allow your flesh to fool you into thinking that the life you see is what is true. He alone is the Truth.

> He longs to possess all of you — including your mind.

Every day you can build for eternity. Every day your fallen nature can be more transformed into His likeness as you learn to take captive every thought, bringing it into obedience to the spirit within. You may be a stay-at-home mom, or you may be an evangelist to thousands, but Jesus is looking at the spirit within you, and He desires to strengthen, enlarge, and undergird it. He desires, by His Truth, to completely transform the lies within your fallen nature. Some lies are personal lies, some are cultural lies, some are simply "human" lies.

"For whom He foreknew, He also predestined to be conformed to the image of His Son, that He might be the firstborn among many brethren." (Romans 8:29). Being conformed to the image of Jesus Christ takes time and process. Be patient with yourself and others; He is patient with you. There was only one Perfect One, and yet He calls us to be perfect like Him. (Matthew 5:48). This is your Call, your purpose. I urge you: do not allow one more day to "slip" by without seeking to answer His Call.

SCRIPTURE
Further References: Matthew 5:48; Romans 8:28-29, 12:2; Galatians 5:16-17, 24-25; 1 Peter 1:13-16; 1 John 5:20

JOURNAL ENTRY:

Now I see that He is raising me to a level of faith to understand and see all things from His perspective. How He aches for His people, their hearts, their attention and their love. How He longs for union with us, for this truly is why we were created! We run here and we run there, and all the time He is saying "My child, I am within you." The Kingdom of God is in our midst, when we dwell in Him. Apart from Him, we are separate individuals moving with distinct identities. Oh, that we would realize that it is all of us together who will fulfill Eph 2:22 "in whom you also are being built together into a dwelling of God in the Spirit."

Childlike Simplicity

O, how we love you, Lord! Yet, we can become so fogged up in many deep things that we forget the first commandment to love you with all of our heart, mind, and soul.

But how simple that commandment is — so simple that it has been designated to reside within the heart of a child. You tell us that we must become like little children. You say that the kingdom of heaven belongs to such as these. Little children are not fogged up with lofty concepts, or great ideas, or too many responsibilities. They live in the present, moment by moment. They are born with the gift of trust. They know their parents and they cling to them. They relish in security. They laugh and play.

With growth comes responsibility and independence.

Give us back our childlike simplicity that we lost over the years when we were wounded and began to build walls to protect ourselves. Or perhaps it was when we grew up and became self-sufficient enough not to need an adult to lean upon.

With growth comes responsibility and independence. Too much of these creates a long road between us and the cross. Sure, we are saved, but we continually resist running to the cross because of the self-sufficiency ingrained within our nature. A child is not self-sufficient. A child does not know pressure. A child doesn't know about achieving. A child does know about unquestioning trust.

O Lord, take the yoke that adulthood brings to us within our modern individualistic society. Set us free, Lord, and let us learn the art of childlikeness. Teach us what it means to be mature believers, yet children of the Father. Set us free from the temptation to view our circumstances as an indicator of Your love for us. Deliver us from the lies that prohibit us from loving You as children — lies of perfectionism, lies of independence, self-sufficiency, and inability to trust.

The Training Ground

If you feel as though all the armies of hell have been unleashed against you, then kneel down in praise to God. The adversary deems you a worthy opponent! How else do you think a soldier is prepared for the battlefield? There must be some kind of a spiritual boot camp in which we acquire the Discipline, the Fortitude, and the Tenacity required to go to war. "Praise be to the Lord my Rock, Who trains my hands for battle, my fingers for war." (Psalm 144:1).

The training ground is hard. Many drop out.

The training ground is hard. Many drop out. Some are badly wounded; others are simply disillusioned; and others are unscratched, yet totally ineffective, because they spiritually compromise at the onset, causing Satan no threat whatsoever.

Satan's energy is mostly targeted on the power sources of Christ. Those warriors who are proven effective will learn how to advance the most during Satan's most aggressive periods. (Genesis 50:19-20). In what would be one of Satan's greatest victories (and your greatest defeat) lies the opportunity for the opposite — God's greatest victory. God's glory can rest more fully on you in your weakness.

Overcomers

Those who are overcomers have known despair. They have known the Dark Night of the Soul. Don't you see that, if it was easy to become an overcomer, the name would lose its entire meaning? Overcoming has nothing to do with feelings. It has nothing to do with sight. It has everything to do with the invisible Savior who lives within. He may be invisible. He may be intangible. But His promises are not. And He promises to reward all who overcome.

If you desire to be an overcomer, then watch your circumstances. Watch your "life" as you see it begin to unravel. Watch tremendous difficulties and warfare of intense nature come your way. Watch the temptation to "give up" press itself heavily upon your soul. Know that God's finest have been where you are. Just because you are in a struggle for your very life, you are not losing any ground. It all depends upon your view of your self. In your self, you are nothing. But inside of your feeble frame lies the power of a resurrection Savior. This is where you must place your trust. This is where your hope — and your power to endure — reside.

> Just because you are in a struggle for your very life, you are not losing any ground.

Today, if you are surrounded by difficulties that threaten to devour your very life, plant your entire self upon this Truth. Know that today in eternity your crown is being carved.

SCRIPTURES
"Be faithful until death, and I will give you the crown of life." (Revelation 2:10).
"Behold, I am coming quickly! Hold fast what you have, that no one may take your crown." (Revelation 3:11)

Further References: Romans 8:11; 2 Corinthians 4:10-12; Hebrews 6:19

What is Joy?

Joy is hearing my Bridegroom's voice, above all the other voices of the world and my human nature. Joy is seeing — truly seeing — the eternal goal that my Father has for me, just as Jesus endured the cross and all its sorrows with the inner knowledge that nothing but this plan would accomplish eternal redemption for all of God's children.

Joy is what I experience when I am crushed by the Lord's hand, knowing that this and this alone is what will keep me from exalting myself. Joy is mine when I know, heart, mind, and soul, that God is for me and not against me, that He is radically and passionately for me more than I could ever imagine!

I feel joy when I know that God is changing my heart, removing walls of fear and replacing them with love; when I know beyond a shadow of a doubt that all my springs are in Him, and there is no frailty or weakness that can ever stop His power.

I experience joy when I sense the sufficiency of His grace in the midst of a terrible trial; and see Him provide my needs after I purposely release all of my efforts to do so; and know my life is not my own, but my steps are ordered by divine love.

Joy is mine when I know, truly know, that nothing or no one can cancel out God's purpose and plan for my life.

SCRIPTURE
Further References: Job 42:1; Psalm 16:5-11; Isaiah 14:24, 27; 46:9-10; John 3:29; 4:14, 18; Romans 8:28-39; 2 Corinthians 12:9-10; Hebrews 12:2; 1 Peter 5:6

Can You Become Like a Child?

"At that time Jesus answered and said, 'I thank You, Father, Lord of heaven and earth, that You have hidden these things from the wise and prudent and have revealed them to babes. Even so, Father, for it seemed good in Your sight.'" (Matthew 11:25-26).

Why do we act as if we are wise? Why do we act as if we have it all together? What is so hard about being a child? Is it that we are not in control? Is it because we are called to live in the moment, trust in the unseen Arms, not giving thought for our problems, concerns, or tomorrows? Is this too uncertain for us? Or perhaps too frightening? Some of us carry unseen wounds that happened to us when we were children. So, as children, we weren't given the luxury to trust. Some of us were abused by those who were supposed to protect us, and as a result, our concept of trust has become perverted.

> What is so hard about being a child?

What a travesty to the heart of God! How He longs to love us and care for us, but we cannot follow His command to be like children. "Unless you change and become like little children, you will never enter the kingdom of heaven." (Matthew 18:3, NIV). Our defense mechanisms have become our safety, and yet they block the TRUE SAFETY of His love. A child in the arms of a true father has absolute trust and total dependence. Let the heart of our Father God heal you where you missed out. Let Him take you back to being a child, and allow Him to renew your mind with His Truth. Then you will be able to follow His command to be like a child. Indeed, then you will enter the Kingdom of Heaven now, as a present reality, and not only as a future hope.

Running Unencumbered

At all costs, prayer and communication must be maintained. Otherwise, we open ourselves up to the enemy of our souls. The flesh is weak, and although the spirit may indeed be very willing, a moment of fleshly decision, emotion, or reaction can be very costly. We must recognize at the onset that anything alive within our self is going to block the progress of God's Holy Spirit. We must run unencumbered or we will not "run" at all. Self must be conquered, and the only way to conquer it is through the cross. Self cannot be reasoned with, rationalized, or justified. It has no choice but to die … if it truly wants to live where Jesus desires it to live. "Now we have received, not the spirit of the world, but the spirit who is from God, that we might know the things freely given to us by God." (1 Corinthians 2:12).

Dying involves great pain, but if we as the church are going to stand out in the midst of the world, how do we do so? How does the light of Jesus Christ shine forth from our hearts and homes to attract the lost around us? Once we are saved, we must diligently set out to embrace the cross of Jesus Christ. Any self left will only open the door for the enemy's attempts to thwart us from God's best. We have not yet begun to move in the power of God as He has ordained for the last days.

Those lovers who are now practicing the laying down of their lives and their rights are building the foundation of Godly power. Right now, God, in hiddenness, is preparing the hearts who will lay down their lives hourly and daily with total abandonment.

What we see on the outside will have little to do with the inner man or woman. In fact, the outside is so often illusory that those who map their progress by what is visible will miss the ways of God and His awesome workings.

Standing Firm

"Put on the whole armor of God, that you may be able to stand against the schemes of the devil ... that you may be able to withstand in the evil day, and having done all, to stand." (Ephesians 6:11, 13).

Sometimes, all we can do is stand our ground. But sometimes, that is enough, because in the process of holding firm against Satan's attack, we are actually being prepared for future battle, as well as being strengthened in dependence upon God.

> When God removes His protective hedge from us, it is a challenge to see whether our armor is intact.

We may panic when we sense an attack of Satan, and try to "get busy" to get out of it, when actually we need to "get still" and find our strength in God. Psalm 91:4 says that God's faithful promises are our armor and our protection. We must cover ourselves with Gods' promises. Our minds, emotions, and our bodies must be bathed with the words of assurance regarding the faithfulness of God, and this shall be our armor.

God's faithfulness alone can enable us to firmly withstand assaults from our greatest enemies in the physical realm. Those assaults only serve to test our armor and make sure it is of the highest standard.

When God removes His protective hedge from us, it is a challenge to see whether our armor is intact. Are there any holes in it? Have we been adding new arsenals to our sword? Is our shield of faith expansive enough to cover the type of permission that God gave Satan regarding His servant Job?

Paul uses the words "stand firm" four times in this passage, perhaps to depict the gravity of the situation. It is one thing to stand firm when you are full of zeal, energy, and enthusiasm. It is another thing to stand firm when your energies are taxed, your external world is caving in, or you are being called upon to "bear up under" trials of great intensity.

It is then that "standing firm" becomes much more than defending oneself against the enemy. It is causing your roots to plummet deep down into the soil of God's love and faithfulness.

It seems we only dig down when we are hemmed in on all sides and have nowhere to escape. It is then that God's soldiers are being trained in the most powerful way yet. On the outside, it may appear that nothing is being accomplished, but on the inside, He is equipping them for battle of the most aggressive kind.

JOURNAL ENTRY:

It is when all the props are pulled out that we realize what our life is based upon. If our life is based upon our external identity we will be found empty. If it is based upon the person of Jesus Christ, we will be unmoved even if the landscape of our lives is turned upside down. There is no doubt that every child of God can and must grow stronger in the Lord. You and Him. Just you and Him. There cannot be enough emphasis upon this ultimate relationship of friendship and love!

Who is Willing to Drink the Cup?

A lot of teaching focuses on victory and the blessings of God. Trials and testing are too quickly labeled "attacks from the enemy" or declared to be Satan's methods of hindering our walk. True, our enemy does attack, and he is always looking for a way to block us from the full purposes of God. But look deeper into the life of one who earnestly seeks the deep purposes of God.

What do the very words of Jesus testify to? They speak of dying to our self, losing our life, picking up the cross. He declares that we are blessed if we are persecuted, we are blessed when we are excluded and insulted, we are blessed when we are hated and our names are rejected as evil, we are blessed when we weep or are poor and hungry.

Jesus doesn't say, "Attacked are you who are persecuted. Attacked are you who weep." Jesus overturned the value structure of the world. What we see as terrible, He says is good. What we are so quick to rebuke, He says is necessary. (Matthew 16:23-25). Jesus doesn't focus on the source of our pain and injustice. He focuses on the individual who undergoes the pain, suffering, mourning, and persecution. He says, "Blessed are *you*." He didn't focus on those who carried out the crucifixion. He focused on what was accomplished in the crucifixion. We do not hear Him speak about the ones who handed Him the cup to drink, or the ones who baptized Him through His suffering and death. He speaks of the baptism, but not the baptizers. (Luke 12:50).

James and John asked Jesus to allow each of them to sit in positions of prestige and power at Jesus' side — one at His right hand and one at His left hand — when He comes in all His glory. Jesus' response makes it clear that His beloved disciples were a little misled in their request: "You do not know what you are asking." To attain such honor alongside of Jesus, they had to be willing to undergo the same fate that Jesus Himself would.

Those closest to Him greatly missed the point. Peter is given one of the strongest rebukes throughout the entire Gospels when He tries to tell Jesus that He must not undergo His death. "Get behind Me, Satan! You are a stumbling block to Me; you do not have in mind the things of God, but the things of men." (Matthew 16:23). Then turn back to the suffering servant Job, who was afflicted at the hands of the Adversary. But does God speak to Job about Satan? No. He shows Job how limited his understanding is. His rebuke is similar to Jesus'. "Who is this that darkens My counsel with words without knowledge?" (Job 38:2).

My friends, could it be that we often miss the point, too? Could it be that we, like Peter, have in mind the things of men and not of God? Do we seek blessing and honor with God more than we seek to walk the path? Do we focus more on taking authority over the evil one than on submitting to God's authority? It is easier to blame trials on Satan than to recognize that God may be using him as a tool to baptize us with the same baptism as Jesus'. Perhaps it is easier to attack outside of ourselves than to submit inwardly with a humility that only Jesus carried. Are we too focused on "victory" and not enough on the path that Jesus walked? (Matthew 16:23-25).

I pray today that we would become willing to walk this path. May we seek to honor Jesus by purposefully losing our lives and not shrinking back from the cross He gives us, even if it is at the hand of His enemy. Let us recognize that the enemy is often God's tool for bringing us deeper into Him. There is never a moment that the Master is not in charge.

Unattractive Gifts

This morning, while I was meditating on the goodness of God, I felt the Lord speak to me about one facet of His "goodness."

We tend to think of goodness as giving "good things," but God began to show me that out of His goodness, He gives us what is best. And sometimes "the best" comes to us in ways we would have great difficulty describing as good. Many times when God seems to be the "least" good to us, He is actually giving us some of His choicest morsels.

> Sometimes "the best" comes to us in ways we would have great difficulty describing as good.

Some of the best gifts come wrapped in the ugliest packages, but, because we are so prone to look with our visual eyes, our first reaction tends to be "How can anything good come out of this?"

But God, in His lovingkindness, reaches out to us in the midst of some very "unpretty" gifts. As we willingly accept what God gives us, we can begin to unwrap the layers of packaging together with Him. His goal is always that we would get to the center of the gift, and the center always has a treasure of eternal significance. The only problem is that we, in our flesh, often receive our homely gift from God and immediately cringe at the thought of embracing it! Yet God calls us not only to embrace it, but to carry it until His time of unwrapping is due. Sometimes, He'll lead us to unwrap one layer at a time, carrying our gift for periods in between. But with each layer, the glow within can be seen more brightly.

God's heart is grieved when we resist His uncomely packages, choosing to "ignore" them, "deny" them, or, worse yet, "rebuke" them. God invites us to commune with Him at every turn in life, and sometimes His most powerful invitations come through heavy, burdensome packages. Some wrapping paper is like sandpaper, cutting and bruising our flesh as we carry it. Some packages are almost humiliating in appearance, and our Lord asks us to carry them in public, without being ashamed of what He has given us. Some packages are so heavy, we are forced to enlist help from others, thus surrendering our self-sufficiency and pride.

"Do not be deceived, my beloved brethren. Every good gift and every perfect gift is from above, and comes down from the Father of lights, with whom there is no variation or shadow of turning." (James 1:16-17).

Oh, Father, give us Your wisdom to see that everything You give us is good. Release us from our earthly vision and temporal judgment. Give us greater grace, O Lord, to receive all You seek to give us, especially the difficult gifts. Enlarge our understanding, so we may see, rather than be deceived. You, O Lord, never change. You are absolute and perfect in Your love for us, and You select the gift we need at the precise time we need it. And even though the gifts may vary from pleasant to painful, all of them are consistently "perfect" because they come from You. In Your blessed and holy name we pray, Amen.

Coming Forth as Gold

Job 23:10: "But He knows the way that I take; when He has tested me, I shall come forth as gold." (Job 23:10).

As believers, we must be careful not to assume that we know what God is doing in the lives of one another.

> Wisdom is only found in God and in the fear of Him.

There is a definite purpose for trials as a means of purification, but there is also a testing of our faith that can carry the appearance of trials. God tested Job to show that Job was pure gold. There is no doubt that Job was different after his suffering. He used to be a man who knew God and, like his friends, probably had much counsel to offer to others about God. But after his painful testing, he was a man who had seen God face to face. "My ears had heard of You but now my eyes have seen You." (Job 42:5, NIV). A necessary part of Job's faith was a fear of God who does what He pleases. "But He is unique, and who can make Him change? And whatever His soul desires, that He does. For He performs what is appointed for me, and many such things are with Him. Therefore I am terrified at His presence; when I consider this, I am afraid of Him." (Job 23:13-15).

In contrast, his friends tried to make God predictable. They claimed to know why Job was suffering. They spoke about God with accurate Scriptural knowledge, but they failed to speak from a personal knowledge of the living God. "My wrath is aroused against you and

JOURNEYS OF A WARRIOR POET

180

your two friends, for you have not spoken of Me what is right, as my servant Job has." (Job 42:7).

Believers, wisdom is only found in God and in the fear of Him. God does what He pleases. He cannot be manipulated to perform, nor is He in debt to us. It pleased Him to allow Satan the liberty to practically annihilate Job's entire life. All this so that Job — a man who feared God and shunned evil already (Job 1:1) — would have a personal, revolutionary concept of what it truly means to fear God.

How many of us could prove to be such worthy vessels? At what point might we give up believing that our Father of love and mercy was still our Father of love and mercy? At what point might the feelings of utter abandonment take their toll within our finite minds? "Nevertheless, when the Son of Man comes, will He really find faith on the earth?" (Luke 18:8).

Lord Jesus, give us discernment as we walk in our finite minds and yet long to grasp the infinite. Give us eyes of faith and spiritual understanding. Take away our presumption, Lord. Show us how spiritually arrogant we can be. Give us, O Lord, a humble, reverent fear of You. And give us also a faith that will prove to be as gold if You should ask of us something that we would never have imagined. And may this faith be the kind that You will be pleased to find when You return as the Righteous Judge.

JOURNAL ENTRY:
Nothing can stop the work of the Living God.

Discarding Our Lack of Faith

There must come a point in our Christian walk when we are ready to discard our lack of faith and our human reasoning.

Have you come to this point? Has a sense of discontentment been awakened within you? Are you dissatisfied with the way you have been living — when waters of life are available for your drinking? (John 7:37-38). Why allow yourself to be contained by your five senses, when the One who lives within you is ready to lead you onward?

When we depend upon what we see, hear, feel, taste, or smell, we actually enclose ourselves within the walls of unbelief. Unbelief knows nothing about the walk of faith that Peter took when he ventured out to meet Jesus upon the turbulent sea. We are quick to point out how Peter failed when he took his eyes off his Lord. Yet, Peter was the only disciple to exhibit the boldness of faith to even step out of the boat.

We must recognize that unbelief is the norm, not the exception, within our Christian mindset and churches today. Truly we are better off than unbelievers, for we can attest to the peace and joy we have in Christ Jesus. But are we missing out on the great Truth of the Almighty God who dwells within: that there are no limits, no regions, no walls to contain His majesty?

Believing Jesus for eternal life is one thing. But it is entirely another thing to believe Him for all our provisions, including complete inner healing and absolute freedom from the world, the flesh, and the devil. Yet, to those who hunger for more than freedom, He offers the opportunity to experience the miraculous. "Most assuredly, I say to you, he who believes in Me, the works that I do he will do also; and greater works than these he will do, because I go to My Father."

(John 14:12). Greater things than Jesus did! Who would want to miss out on this promise?

"Because you have seen Me, you have believed; blessed are those who have not seen and yet have believed." (John 20:29). Brothers and sisters, if we were to examine our hearts and our attitudes, could we call ourselves "believers" in every single aspect of our lives? Or would we, in actuality, be forced to admit that we are in part "doubters"?

"In Him we live and move and have our being." (Acts 17:28). We may attest to this Truth, but do we center our lives around it? The Spring of living water cannot be contained within the walls of unbelief and still live. It will simply cease to flow.

Jesus is calling us to step out on the sea of faith as Peter had the courage to do, to renounce our belief system that holds us in bondage, to claim with Paul that indeed "we walk by faith, not by sight." (2 Corinthians 5:7). But before we can claim this, we must first confess the areas where this is not true. Where do we walk by sight, sense, or hearing, and not by faith? Paul states that as long as we are at home in the body we are away from the Lord. (2 Corinthians 5:6).

Unbelief is a stronghold. Are you at home within this stronghold? If you are, in any area of your life, then you are denying yourself the living water. What good is all of our knowledge if we do not unleash the power of the One within? Let us unleash the dormant power of Jesus Christ within our lives, our homes, our churches, and our land!

SCRIPTURE
Further References: John 11:40; Ephesians 3:20

Transformation by Trials

There comes a point when we would be wise to welcome God's trials into our lives.

The reason lies in our human proclivity towards sin. It is no lie that we exist within a fallen nature. Though our spirit has been made alive and the living Word now dwells within us, we still move within a fallen nature. It is interesting to see people (and they do not even have to be believers) go through deep, dark valleys, and, as a consequence, the things that used to matter to them — having their own way, needing their opinion to be heard, needing recognition from others — do not matter any more.

> What kind of person is the indwelling Christ producing in you?

They may have learned, through tremendous difficulties, to shed the outer layers of the garments they embody: superficiality, pettiness, self-centeredness, phoniness. Something about trials takes us deeper into what is true, what really counts. "Whatever things are true, whatever things are noble, whatever things are just, whatever things are pure, whatever things are lovely, whatever things are of good report, if there is any virtue and if there is anything praiseworthy — meditate on these things." (Philippians 4:8).

Paul tells us to put off our old self, "which grows corrupt according to its deceitful desires, and be renewed in the spirit your mind, and that you put on the new man which was created according to God, in true righteousness and holiness." (Ephesians 4:22-24).

What kind of person is the indwelling Christ producing in you? Are you obedient to put off what you need to, and put on what God asks you to? If you are, then you are living as children of light, finding out what pleases the Lord, and exposing the deeds of darkness. (Ephesians 5:8-11).

Those of us who have been believers for a number of years should be quick to address any remnants of the old nature within us. For example, we are called to put off falsehood and speak truthfully to one another, and this is exactly what we are to do. Our relationships should be aglow with the light of Jesus' love and the glory of God. Sacrifice should be the norm and not the exception. "Live a life of love, just as Christ loved us and gave Himself up for us as a fragrant offering and sacrifice to God." (Ephesians 5:2, NIV).

As Paul says, "Among you there must not be even a hint of sexual immorality, or of any kind of impurity, or of greed, because these are improper for God's holy people." (Ephesians 5:3, NIV). Not even a hint!

Beloved, we have the indwelling Christ — we cannot afford to tolerate passivity towards our old self! We grieve the Holy Spirit when we allow ourselves to adopt the attitude that our flesh desires, especially when other believers hold the same attitude. Our hearts become hardened by the deceitfulness of sin, and in essence, we turn away from the living God. (Hebrews 3:12-14; Jeremiah 17:9).

Does it take a trial to shake us out of our lukewarm mindsets and plant us firmly into the calling we have received? (Ephesians 4:1; 2 Thessalonians 1:11). If so, then praise God! I praise God that He loved me enough to take me into the valley of suffering. The things that used to matter do not matter anymore, and my outer life is more in accord with what is true and real.

> Does it take a trial to shake us out of our lukewarm mindsets and plant us firmly into the calling we have received?

No, my trials are not over, and certainly I am not yet perfected. My hope is that my heart is being changed in the process, that my faith is growing more and more, and that my love for God's children and His lost ones is increasing. (2 Thessalonians 1:3-5). I pray that I am loving less from my human nature (my personal convenience), and more from the love of God overflowing from the indwelling presence of His Son. "We are bound to thank God always for you, brethren, as it is fitting, because your faith grows exceedingly, and the love of every one of you all abounds toward each other, so that we ourselves boast of you among the churches of God for your patience and faith in all your persecutions and tribulations that you endure." (2 Thessalonians 1:3-4).

JOURNAL ENTRY:
Our capacity to care for others is limited, or expanded by our own capacity for suffering.

Walking in Darkness

Sometimes God wants us to walk in darkness with little or no return from Him. During the Dark Night of the Soul, we are stripped of everything we have depended upon … even hearing His voice.

I believe it is one of His ultimate acts of lovingkindness when He withdraws even His presence. Left to ourselves, are we going to fend for ourselves? Or are we going to pour our hearts out in longing for Him and wait for Him to come to us?

When God withdraws from us and we are left alone, we can sense the futility of the flesh and the barren nature of the soul left to its own desires. The second part of John 15:5 must become a reality in our lives if we are truly to understand the power of God in which our Father desires us to walk. The flesh is so strong, and God is in the business of weaning us from all that comes by way of nature. We must come to the point of utter helplessness and poverty of spirit to experience His power. He stands by patiently until we are crying out for Him with every fiber of our being.

> We must come to the point of utter helplessness and poverty of spirit to experience His power.

SCRIPTURE
"He does not delight in the strength of the horse; He takes no pleasure in the legs of a man. The Lord takes pleasure in those who fear Him, in those who hope in His mercy." (Psalm 147:10-11)

"Therefore with joy you will draw water from the wells of salvation." (Isaiah 12:3)

The Lion of Judah

I have made up my mind, I am going to believe. Against all evidence to the contrary, I am going to believe! I am going to believe in the power of God within me. I am not going to believe in the world, or believe in what I know and can see and can feel. I am going to believe in what I do not yet know (in experience), in what I do not yet see and in what I do not yet feel.

> All the enemy can do is attempt to hinder us in our destiny.

I am ready to cross the Jordan. I am ready to receive the new identity God wants to give me. I am ready for a paradigm shift in my thinking, in the way I relate to reality. I am ready for the *mind of Christ* to settle upon me. The fearsome and the fearless mind of Christ. I will no longer move by fear but I will move by faith. I am ready to overcome my last and final obstacle causing fear in my life. I am ready to face the enemy head-on, for he is no foe to the One who lives within me. Raise up the Lion of Judah, oh Lord, raise it up within us so that we will begin to fight for our destiny! All the enemy can do is attempt to hinder us in our destiny, but part of our walking in it depends upon our forcefulness in pursuing it!

JOURNAL ENTRY:

It seems that God allows us to be pressed down from the outside in order that we will rise up on the inside. Being crushed on the outside will necessitate a rising up of the Spirit within. The Spirit has no choice but to rise up in forcefulness or else it will die. There is the danger of spiritual death of course, and that is why the enemy takes his chance. One person may rise up in true spiritual advancement while the other may shrink back in fear and unbelief!

Little Children

God calls us to be wise and discerning. But He also calls us to be like little children.

What is it about a little child that brings joy to our hearts? It's a trust that doesn't say, "Prove yourself to me." It's a joy that is not based on position, power, or purpose. It's a joy that a two-year-old expresses when he says, "Mommy, watch me run!" He's happy to be alive, and excited to bask in his mother's love.

God calls us to be wise and discerning.

But He also calls us to be like little children.

What if we were to have such a gratitude for our salvation that we would exclaim, "Jesus, You have freed my restraints! Watch me run!" No performance, no work, just pure joy in what He has done for us. I wonder what joy He would feel to watch us run.

SCRIPTURE
"I run in the path of Your commands, for You have set my heart free." (Psalm 119:32, NIV)

"And He said, 'I tell you the truth, unless you change and become like little children, you will never enter the kingdom of heaven.'" (Matthew 18:3, NIV)

Do You Know His Voice?

The world says, "Listen to your heart." Jesus says, "Listen to My voice." The world says, "Follow your gut." Jesus says, "Follow your Shepherd." "He calls His own sheep by name and leads them out … His sheep follow Him because they know His voice. But they will never follow a stranger; in fact, they will run away from him because they do not recognize a stranger's voice." (John 10:4-5).

> Are you cultivating your intimacy with Jesus to such an extent that you know His voice immediately when He calls?

Do you know His voice? If you do, then you will follow Him. You will come in and go out and find pasture, and have life to the full.

But you will never follow a stranger. In fact, you will run form a stranger's voice because you do not recognize it. And this is your protection. The stranger cannot make you follow him, and he cannot imitate the voice of the Shepherd. So, you see, you need not fear the stranger. You need only run from him.

While a stranger cannot force you to follow him, Jesus will not force you to follow. John 10:4 says, "He goes on ahead of them." The Palestinian shepherd led his sheep, he did not drive them. Believers, Jesus stands in front of us. He doesn't stand behind and push us. He expects us to follow. Why wouldn't we? He is the one who offers us abundant life. Why would we follow the stranger's voice? He comes only to steal, kill, and destroy. Why would we entertain the thought of following his voice, if we know the result will be death? (James 1:14-15, Romans 8:6).

It all boils down to discernment. If we are not able to recognize the Shepherd's voice, then we might be tricked. We know that any good thief is a master at stealth and deception. If he attempts to rob a house in the middle of the day, then he'll more likely be seen. No, he'll come out at night and probably sneak in a side door, not in the front where there would be an open view. He'll probably even have a disguise on, for he won't want to give away his identity.

It is interesting to see that the offer of abundant life, once accepted from Jesus, is ours to maintain. We maintain it by following Jesus' voice. And in order to follow it, we must know it. We must also know that a good thief will go after the best treasure he can find. So if you have a "real good" taste of Jesus' abundant life, you better have a "real good" grasp of His voice, because the thief is going to try to get what you have.

Are you growing in your discernment? Are you cultivating your intimacy with Jesus to such an extent that you know His voice immediately when He calls — and you know the counterfeit just as quickly? "But solid food is for the mature, who by constant use have trained themselves to distinguish good from evil." (Hebrew 5:14, NIV).

I pray that if you have been in the shepherd's fold for a while, you can say with honesty and sincerity that you have been trained to recognize His voice. I pray that you are living the abundant life because you follow His voice and not the voices of the world, your loved ones, or your flesh. If this is the case for you, believer, then rejoice! The thief has no part of your life! You have only the joy of knowing that your are living the life that Jesus came to give. (John 15:11). I encourage you — no matter what your age — to know His voice and follow it so that you may have life, and have it to the full.

Become One With Your Purpose

There is grace in the dying. There is power in the process. There is purification in the pain. Raise your eyes, then, as true heroes and heroines, and recognize the battle you are in. Do not be dismayed, even though the stakes are high. There is not, and never will be, any greater purpose worth living for.

Long ago, when you began your quest for purpose, did you know it would have cost you so much? Did you imagine it was something you simply "stepped into," or did you realize that it would take every single bit of your very life, with nothing saved for yourself, but all given for the sake of the cause?

You see, you must become ONE with your purpose — there is no separation between who you are and what you are called to do. The redeemer redeems, the restorer restores, the deliverer delivers, the healer heals, the beautifier beautifies. But before you walk forward in the fullness of your purpose, you must come into union with the battle that is being fought in the spirit.

The battles will bring forth the gold in you and define who you are, as long as you do not compromise in the midst of them. Simply enduring trials is not enough for the ones who are called to walk in the footsteps of the Almighty. Those who shine in the midst of great trial are those who will move forward in His glory. Battles define what is in the heart of every man and woman, and those who move forward are those who fearlessly face the enemy without compromise. Remember, it will take all of you. All of your mind, all of your heart, all of your strength. A great price has been paid for the gift of your salvation. But there is a great cost to walk in the fullness of your purpose. You must press in to see your destiny revealed.

The Masterpiece of the Wilderness

One of the main purposes of the wilderness is to bring about a paradigm shift in our thinking. Before the wilderness we are in control of our own life. We basically live our life and we do good things as a Christian, but Christ is not the Sovereign Lord over our life. After the wilderness we are absolutely dependent upon Jesus. We are simply and purely, not our own. He is the Sovereign Lord over our lives. We do as He wills. Even if our will may assert itself for a moment, our mind is renewed to the point where we can still discern His will and therefore walk in it. This is the renewing of our minds, which is the paradigm shift.

Also, during the wilderness, our dividedness or fragmentation comes together. It is actually through external fragmentation, when our life begins to fall apart, that our internal fragmentation is revealed. Therefore it is a good thing when we "fall apart," because then the Lord can begin to piece us back together as a new creation "in Him." We will be pieced together by His voice speaking truth and light to our broken identities. Broken because they were formed in a broken world and had words spoken into them by "broken people." Therefore, healing occurs through the process of the Living Word being spoken into our depths, revealing in true reality who we are and who we were created to be.

> We will be pieced together by His voice speaking truth and light to our broken identities.

The wilderness is actually a masterpiece in design!

Forceful Men and Women

"From the days of John the Baptist until now, the kingdom of heaven has been forcefully advancing, and forceful men lay hold of it." (Matthew 11:12).

Forceful men and women don't say, "I want the things of eternity." Simply desiring the things of eternity is not enough. They must have the things of eternity! There is a cry from deep within them that cannot be stopped from rising upward. It burns for a release. It's the divine call set aflame that burns and rises in passion towards the source from which it began. It is the eternal cry within every man or woman who tastes the wonder of God and knows beyond any doubt that there is no peace or no purpose apart from this Divine Love which draws him or her heavenward.

> Forceful men and women are messy men and women, because they know the cross.

Forceful men and women are messy men and women, because they know the cross. Crucifixion, by its nature, is messy and violent, but this is no deterrent to forceful men and women. They're after the glory, and anything they encounter is a small price to pay compared to the glory of the prize they're after. ·

Forceful men and women live for God, for His sake. They have no real desire to receive anything. Even though He has many good gifts to offer, they just want to receive Him and be united with Him. The eternal song within them cries out not just for a release, but for completion, and He is their completion. He and He alone will satisfy them. The must see His face. They must feel His embrace. They must sing this song to the nations. They cannot be kept quiet; they cannot be held down. Crucifixion only multiplies their yearning. It only increases their hunger.

Who are these men and women? They are the ones prophesied about by Jesus Christ Himself. They are the men and women who take the kingdom of God by force, and bring it right down in our midst. They are the ones who refuse to back down to the prince of darkness. They are the ones who will redefine the face of this planet. Some of them don't yet know who they are. They don't know they have a song, for the world has told them they do not have a voice. They don't understand their restlessness. They don't understand their hunger at the end of the day.

These are the ones who must be awakened. These are the ones who must be retrieved from the false freedom that others are satisfied with. Go out and find them. Find your song within you and sing it with all your heart.

Awaken the forceful men and women within your midst. You are one of them. They are all around you.

JOURNAL ENTRY:

It is often said that if we delight ourselves in the Lord, He will give us the desires of our heart. (Psalm 37:4). Truly, if we delight ourselves in the Lord Jesus Christ, if we seek Him with fervor and single mindedness, He will transform our heart into a heart that desires only Him! So the Scripture is therefore fulfilled, He gives us Himself. He alone is the desire of our heart!

The Power of God's Peace

The peace of God rules in the midst of His enemies. It does not fight, it does not cower in fear, it does not shrink back. It, quite simply, rules. So, dearest believer, you must never believe that the enemy has been allowed to get the best of you. If you are united with Jesus in the heavenly realm, you have the promise that His peace will always be with you. In the midst of the battle, His peace will never leave its post. In the midst of the enemy fighting for ground, His peace never stops ruling for even one second.

You would do well to remind yourself that this truth is not negotiable. It is as solid as the cross, and its fortress is impenetrable. If the Sovereign Lord has given the enemy permission to encroach upon your life, then you must plant your feet on His bedrock of peace. His peace is always in control, and His peace will always conquer.

> His peace is always in control, and His peace will always conquer.

"And the peace of God, which transcends all understanding, will guard your hearts and your minds in Christ Jesus." "To guard" is a military concept depicting a sentry standing watch. God's "protective custody" of those who are in Christ Jesus extends to the core of their beings. What an assurance! Not only does God's peace guard and protect, but it goes on to do more — it rules. "You prepare a table before me in the presence of my enemies." (Psalm 23:5).

The peace of God is never threatened. It takes the time to relax and refresh us in the midst of our enemies. Call your enemy's bluff by declaring to him the truth on which you stand. Nothing will infuriate him more than reminding him that his time is short in the course leading up to his sealed destiny. "And the God of peace will soon crush Satan under your feet." Romans 16:20. Remember, He said "soon." And remember, your feet will be the instrument He uses.

Are you in need of reassurance today? Are you on the verge of discouragement or defeat? Then let His peace draw you into the inner recesses of your spirit, where His Spirit dwells unscathed and untouched by the enemy's claws, where all that matters is there — the constancy of His love and the certainty of His purposes.

SCRIPTURE
Further References: 1 Samuel 2:9; John 10:28-29; 1 Peter 1:5

JOURNAL ENTRY:

I fought a lot of battles this week. I won some of them, and I lost some of them. But as I sat back and reflected on the week, I felt that the Lord told me, "You'll learn more lessons from losing than winning." I believe the supreme lesson was that of dependence upon the Lord and absolute powerlessness apart from Him. He impressed upon me the humility that it takes not to cover up your losses but to expose them for what they are! In the exposing, He can transform them. What a beautiful aspect of His redemption — even in our losses, mistakes, shortcomings, weaknesses — He brings victory! In Christ, victory is assured because He transforms us in our weaknesses and defeats as well as our victories. As long as we expose them to His light, He brings the good out of them! He is always redeeming us — calling forth our inner man to greater and greater maturity in Him!

Violent Approach

The true self must be set free from the compulsive self. The compulsive self is driven by busyness, always focusing on what needs to be done. It moves out of fear and insecurity, and by "what it knows." We are programmed throughout our lives to live and act in a certain way, and radical changes need to be made if we want to truly say, "In Him we live and move and have our being." (Acts 17:28).

> The true self moves only when compelled by love.

The true self moves only when compelled by love. The true self hungers to be heard throughout the busyness of the day and through the many distractions that continually present themselves. Jesus said, "He who has ears to hear, let him hear." (Matthew 11:15). It is a form of violence when the Spirit rises up from within and declares to the ears that are not hearing: "Be still! Do nothing! Realign your life in accordance with the One who dwells within."

When Jesus spoke about the Kingdom of Heaven being taken by violent men and women, He was not speaking about fleshly, physical violence. He was speaking about those who violently deal with the falseness of their own human nature. There is a voice waiting to be heard — and that is the voice of Jesus Christ, spoken to our inner spirit, the true self created in the image of Jesus Himself. This is the self that must take a violent approach against the ways of its outer nature.

Every individual is unique in the eyes of Father God. Every individual is unique in the ways of his or her compulsive self. What is wrong for me by the Spirit of the Lord, may be right for someone else by the same Spirit. God has designed us so we will not walk in conformity to one another, but in obedience to His voice and His voice alone.

Come, take a violent approach to your words, your thoughts, your ways of living. Do not accept them as the way your Lover made you. He made you to walk with Him as you dwell in Him and receive His words as your lifeline. Come away today, beloved, and hear the voice of Him who calls you from deep within. Hear Him, be quick to respond, and allow Him to take you further into the beloved one He has created you to be.

Quest for Freedom

Sometimes the greatest persecution will come from the most unlikely people. As you are on this quest for freedom (personal and spiritual), many attacks will come from those who envy your newly found freedom. Remember, if freedom were so easy to step into, everyone would be there right now. Freedom requires an inner violence toward everything that stands in its way. Freedom is not given to those who simply desire it. It is given to those who pursue it with all their heart. The extent to which one enters into this divine freedom will determine the measure of God's love to be released within them. This love is released to those who can properly steward it. Those who walk in total freedom will hold nothing as their own and therefore will allow God's love to drip through them to others as soon as it flows down to them from His throne. These free spirits are nothing but vessels — carriers of the divine treasure of glorious love.

Comfort in Judgments of Purification

The question we must all ask ourselves is this, "Do we meet Jesus in our pain?" Many of us go through difficult circumstances, which were intended to break us, and yet we remain unbroken. Painful circumstances are God's invitation to know Him more by dying to ourselves. When self has no control, when self is being judged, ridiculed or persecuted. Do we fall into the hands of the living God, or do we cling stronger to ourselves in defense and justification?

Judging ourselves to the inner core brings purity to our spiritual eyesight.

It's out of His mercy that God sends judgments, so we may purify ourselves of all that hinders Him from having full operation in us. Do we come out of the pain more filled with Him or more filled with ourselves? The fragrance will be obvious after a time.

Our hearts will be harder or they will be softer. Our eyes will have the filters of insecurity and control, or they will have the filter of divine love. Only when we have judged ourselves will we be able to love others with out judgment.

When we embrace the judgments of God for our own life we are released into a greater capacity to love others with the love of God. Judging ourselves to the inner core brings purity to our spiritual eyesight.

The purer our gaze is, the more clearly we will see God, and the more clearly we will see God in others! And therefore, we can more perfectly love them!

SCRIPTURE
Further References: Ezekiel 18:31; Maathew 5:8, 6:21-22; 1 Corinthians 11:31-32; 1 John 3

JOURNAL ENTRY

Dear Lord, I feel like I am going through a living hell. Please help me Lord. Renew Your hope within me, O Lord. Renew Your love within me, O Lord.

All I can do is trust You, Lord
All I can do is fall into the Arms of the Living God
I'm holding on to nothing, Lord
I'm reaching out to You
I want You and You alone
I will not even glance sideways at anything in the world
My fingers are open, holding onto nothing
My arms are outstretched,
Take it all from me Lord, just give me Yourself!
Just give me You, Jesus
I will die if you do not come to me, Jesus

Oh Lord, I have nothing without You
I am nothing without You

The Fire of God

Therefore since we are receiving a kingdom that cannot be shaken, let us be thankful, and so worship God acceptably with reverence and awe, for our God is a consuming fire. (Hebrews 12:28-29)

Remember the purpose of the fire. The fire purifies and make whole. It burns up all that is in us that is not holy and pure, and sets on fire what is pure and true. It gives us our voice and then releases us to sing. It burns up the veils and reveals the lies. Jesus can then speak truth to the lies, renewing our minds. When our minds are renewed we can hear the voice of the Lord clearly. Lies distort His voice. Lies distort the reality of who we are and the reality of our circumstances. When our minds are renewed we know who we are, and we know to whom we belong. We know and believe and dwell in the love of the Lord Jesus. Therefore, we can discern the voice of the Lord and walk in His will. No longer do we interpret and interact with reality through misperceptions and lies. We are a people of the truth forged within the fires of purification.

> **The fire burns up all that is in us that is not holy and pure, and sets on fire what is pure and true.**

JOURNAL ENTRY:

The question we must all ask ourselves in the midst of activity and momentum in the Kingdom, "Are we growing closer to the Lord? Is He becoming more of our All in All?"

Nothing But Love

Can you imagine not being motivated by anything other than love? Not having an ounce of greed, ambition, insecurity, pride or fear governing your decisions and actions? But doing everything out of Love coming from the love of the Father? Nothing to gain, nothing to lose, all to be given for love, with, and to love. Spilled forth from your very being, your mind having been renewed to the point that nothing directs you or dictates to you other than love?

That is freedom. That is what heaven must be like. I want to experience this on earth!

SCRIPTURE
"We have come to know and have believed the love, which God has for us. God is love, and the one who abides in love abides in God, and God abides in him." (I John 4:7, 12, 16 NAS)

"And do not be conformed to the world, but be transformed by the renewing of your mind, so that you may prove what the will of God is, that which is good and acceptable and perfect." (Romans 12:2 NAS)

JOURNAL ENTRY:

Trials are meant to show us how weak we are, not how strong we are. If we go through a trial without becoming more aware of our own weakness, our personal failings, and the shallowness of our own heart compared to the heart of God, then the trials have missed their purpose.

The True Light

The growth process through the years finds us grabbing hold of "false lights" in order to find our way in life. The true light within us has actually been starved, that is, the true light of Jesus' love and truth. Because it rarely receives it's food to grow, the true light becomes shrouded with layer upon layer of lies that fuels the false light. We need light to live, so if we don't receive the true light, we go out and find the false lights. Also, our culture, our friends, our family, and even our religious customs push the false lights upon us.

So the path to freedom will entail a direct initiative from the hand of God to distill the false lights. They may be taken out all at once, or they may be slowly drained to the point of barely being light at all. "What is this?" the soul exclaims, "I cannot see. I cannot feel love. I am losing all that has given me purpose and meaning in life!"

Soon darkness is upon the soul. In darkness the soul is forced to examine its basic reason for existence. "Who am I?" "Why am I here?" Silence perhaps at first, but then something happens. A flicker of light shines in the darkness. It is a pure light, a beautiful light, something the soul has never seen before. "What is this?" the soul exclaims. The light begins to warm something deep, deep down within the solemn soul. Down it goes, piercing through the layers of falseness, not stopping until it reaches the very center of the individual's heart. Then it speaks a word, a Living Word. Love pours forth from the heart as it begins to feel the true light that has been

> So the path to freedom will entail a direct initiative from the hand of God to distill the false lights.

in this individual for years, only they didn't know it because it had been so starved. Truth pours forth revealing to this soul their true identity, answering their questions they had previously cried out in desperation.

"You are a child of God, dearly and deeply loved. You are beautiful to Me, because I created you in My image. And I am the Sovereign God, Creator of the universe, your Loving Father. I hand picked you for purposes determined only by Me, for purposes only you would fulfill. There is no one like you in all of My Creation. I counseled within My own will about your unique and glorious calling." (Eph. 1:11) "I am yours, your Abba Father, and I want to pour My light into the center of your being where My true light has been in you since birth, for you were created in My image. My light will speak truth to all the lies you have grown up embracing. My light will dispel any desire left within you for the false lights that you have previously depended upon for your meaning and worth. My light will pour forth love within every fiber of your being, so you can do what you were created to do, love Me. For I created you for love and fellowship with Me. What joy, My child, awaits you!"

This is why you are here! Let My light pour forth in you all the love and truth you have been starving for. Let it fill you up, My friend, to the measure of all My fullness. This is My offer to you now. For I am love. I want to draw you deeper and higher into My love. So much awaits you!

SCRIPTURE
Further References: John 1:1-5, 9:16, 12:4-6; Acts 17: 24-28; Ephesians 3:16-20; 1 John 1:1-5

11:11

On the clock: 11:11.

"Truly I say to you, among those born of women there has not arisen anyone greater than John the Baptist! Yet the one who is least in the kingdom of heaven is greater than he." (Matthew 11:11)

I want to believe in the miraculous! I want to believe in the power of the risen Lord living within me, indwelling me for my sole purpose of existence.

Why do I exist? I exist for Him, to love Him, to worship Him and to know Him, and then, to tell the world about Him, or rather, to reveal Him to the world.

> I exist for Him, to love Him, to worship Him and to know Him.

How do I reveal Him? By beginning to allow Him to manifest Himself in my very being, in my life, in my mind, in my heart, in my body. By going through such a death process, that the only life I experience is life in Him. His life, His thoughts, His reflections. His very power healing me, redeeming me, sanctifying me, making me whole. Reclaiming all that has been lost to the darkness and to sin, destroying the works of the devil. Loving Him, worshipping Him, and being with Him will be a life of destroying the devil's works! It will be a life that is true life, for life begets life, it cannot help it!

Oh, that we would partake of His very being. Our thoughts drawing from His thoughts, our emotions drawing from His emotions, our energy drawing from His energy. We are ONE with Him!

The Love of God

The power of God is invincible. The love of God is unstoppable. It will mow down any obstacle that stands in the way of reaching the hearts of God's people. It will go forth violently and call forth the dead from the graves in which they are buried. It will not rest until it claims the desire of it's heart. It will never grow weary. It will never stop flowing from the fountains of heaven itself.

This is the love we seek after. This is the love we desperately need in order to be free. The man-made imitation falls far below the possibility. Even the most spirit-filled men and women only grasp His love for mere moments, but they are as of yet unable to hold onto it and walk in it continuously. To be able to hold onto it takes a heart that has been molded and perfected by the heart of Jesus Himself.

Always pouring out, always reaching after our good, the heart of Jesus longs to be One with His beloved followers. He cherishes them, He woos them on to greatness. For truly "greatness" is only activated according to their conformity with His divine design.

JOURNAL ENTRY:

Do not run from the emptiness to people, places and things. Allow the emptiness to be emptiness and all the loneliness it involves. This is deep purification. The Lord will come and change the emptiness to fullness, but there is an in between waiting time in which great pain exists as well as great temptation. I am in pain because I long to be united with the One for whom I was created. And I am under great temptation to grab hold of something temporary, instead of waiting for the Eternal One to take up his residence in my soul.

JOURNAL ENTRY:

There has been an unraveling process going on — kind of like a peeling of the layers — at times feeling like my skin was being peeled off. "Who am I?" is the pressing question of the moment. Perhaps it has always been the pressing question — the pressure source urging me forward, pressing me into new dimensions of understanding, revelation, and exposure to God's love.

If it is Jesus who dwells within, then in reality, aren't we in pursuit of the revelation of Him who dwells within? Wouldn't this mean a shedding of layers [garments] in order to reach the light within?

Annihilation is only the beginning of transformation.

From the moment we are saved, our inner man is regenerated, but oh! the outer man still exists! It is from this moment that we have the choice to pursue the total revelation of Him who dwells within. To begin the journey is the first step. On the journey, we will shed layers of the old self and we will receive bits and pieces of the new self from the hand of the Lord — little by little, layer by layer, sometimes even chunk by chunk. Basically, we are headed toward our death. Annihilation is only the beginning of transformation.

Once annihilated, we may be tempted to grab hold of some form of life, just because we are desperate for life. But it's really just false life, because it is only a form. True life will come from the source of oil within. It will not take any energy but rather, it will propel you forward. You will know it intuitively — like having a sense that you went somewhere today and you weren't there yesterday. It was in the spirit and not by any effort. It was a work of grace, long awaiting to erupt within the fibres of your being. The Creator placed it in you when He created you and now is the time of coming forth. How He has longed for this time, knowing that much work needed to be done in the process. All the pain and all the suffering that needed to happen in order to purge the outer layers of your carnal nature! Yet, He delighted in the unwrapping, for each step brought Him closer to the diamond within. You are a diamond my child. A diamond of discovery, a diamond of wonder, a diamond of worth!

EPILOGUE

As I close, I want to share a personal story in my own journey. The process of completing this book began in February of 2000. Many editorial complications and setbacks occurred between then and now. While it would appear as though the enemy was "having his way" in such setbacks, that has proven to be far from the truth. The Father of all Glories always ends up receiving the glory in the life of the son or daughter who sets out to seek Him! Any attempt from the enemy to thwart the purposes of God will always prove to fail. God always wins!

You see, in His majesty, God took some "precious time" to carve the message into this "messenger." He was not quite satisfied with my coming into His presence to receive His revelation. He desired to write His Living Word on my heart.

Is He done? No. To be honest, He has just begun. But He has forever captured me!

INDEX OF WRITINGS

PROPHETIC WRITINGS